TUNDRA

TUNDRA

Kolyma River

Indigirka River

Lena River

TAIGA
CONIFEROUS FOREST

Angara River

Lake Baikal

Shilka River

THE SOVIET UNION

THE SOVIET UNION

By The Editors of Time-Life Books

TIME-LIFE BOOKS   ○   ALEXANDRIA, VIRGINIA

COVER: Pedestrians cross Leningrad's
Palace Square. In the background looms
one of the city's most familiar
landmarks — the colonnaded tower of
the Admiralty building, topped by a
gilded spire.

The Soviet Union's official emblem is
shown on page 1, and the national flag
on page 2. Both are decorated with the
hammer and sickle, symbolizing the
union of workers and peasants, and the
red star, a badge of the Soviet state. A
topographic map keyed to environment
and a political map appear on the
endpapers.

Time-Life Books Inc.
is a wholly owned subsidiary of

TIME INCORPORATED

FOUNDER: Henry R. Luce 1898-1967

Editor-in-Chief: Henry Anatole Grunwald
President: J. Richard Munro
Chairman of the Board: Ralph P. Davidson
Corporate Editor: Jason McManus
Group Vice President, Books: Reginald K. Brack Jr.
Vice President, Books: George Artandi

TIME-LIFE BOOKS INC.

EDITOR: George Constable
Executive Editor: George Daniels
Editorial General Manager: Neal Goff
Director of Design: Louis Klein
Editorial Board: Dale M. Brown, Roberta Conlan, Ellen
Phillips, Gerry Schremp, Donia Steele, Rosalind
Stubenberg, Kit van Tulleken, Henry Woodhead
Director of Photography: John Conrad Weiser

PRESIDENT: William J. Henry
Senior Vice President: Christopher T. Linen
Vice Presidents: Stephen L. Bair, Robert A. Ellis, John M.
Fahey Jr., Juanita T. James, James L. Mercer, Wilhelm
R. Saake, Paul R. Stewart, Christian Strasser

LIBRARY OF NATIONS

EDITORS: Dale M. Brown, Martin Mann
Deputy Editor: Phyllis K. Wise
Designer: Raymond Ripper

Editorial Staff for *The Soviet Union*
Associate Editors: Betsy Frankel, Anne Horan, John
Manners, David S. Thomson (text), Jane Speicher
Jordan (pictures)
Researchers: Karin Kinney (principal), Scarlet Cheng,
Denise Li, Paula York-Soderland
Assistant Designer: Robert K. Herndon
Copy Coordinator: Margery duMond
Picture Coordinators: Eric Godwin, Linda Lee
Editorial Assistants: Cathy A. Sharpe, Myrna E. Traylor

Special Contributors: The chapter texts were written by:
Oliver Allen, Ron Bailey, Donald Jackson, Bryce
Walker, Keith Wheeler, and A.B.C. Whipple. *Other
Contributor:* Lydia Preston

Editorial Operations
Design: Ellen Robling (assistant director)
Copy Chief: Diane Ullius
Editorial Operations: Caroline A. Boubin (manager)
Production: Celia Beattie
Quality Control: James J. Cox (director), Sally Collins
Library: Louise D. Forstall

Correspondents: Elisabeth Kraemer-Singh (Bonn);
Margot Hapgood, Dorothy Bacon (London); Miriam
Hsia (New York); Maria Vincenza Aloisi, Josephine du
Brusle (Paris); Ann Natanson (Rome). Valuable
assistance was also provided by: Felix Rosenthal
(Moscow); Christina Lieberman, Lucy T. Voulgaris
(New York).

CONSULTANT

Vadim Medish, Ph.D., Coordinator of
Russian Studies at the American University
in Washington, D.C., grew up in the Soviet
Union. He is the author of numerous
publications on that country.

Library of Congress Cataloguing in Publication Data
Main entry under title:
The Soviet Union.
    (Library of Nations)
    Bibliography: p. 157
    Includes index.
    1. Soviet Union. I. Time-Life Books. II. Series:
Library of Nations (Alexandria, Va.)
DK17.S638   1985   947   85-16334
ISBN 0-8094-5327-4
ISBN 0-8094-5302-9 (lib. bdg.)

CONTENTS

16
Introduction

1 **18**
The Good Life
34 Picture Essay: A Love of the Outdoors

2 **44**
An Immense and Rich Land
58 Picture Essay: Railroad of Young Heroes

3 **66**
A Country of Countries
80 Picture Essay: Peoples at Work

4 **90**
A Long and Violent History
106 Picture Essay: The Living Church

5 **116**
Giants of Imagination
130 Picture Essay: A Blessed Couple

6 **138**
The Omnipotent State

156 **Acknowledgments**
156 **Picture Credits**
157 **Bibliography**
158 **Index**

Instantly recognizable as the symbol of Russia, St. Basil's Cathedral is a combination of nine churches — the central structure surrounded by eight domed

chapels, each honoring saints on whose days Ivan the Terrible won battles against the Tartars.

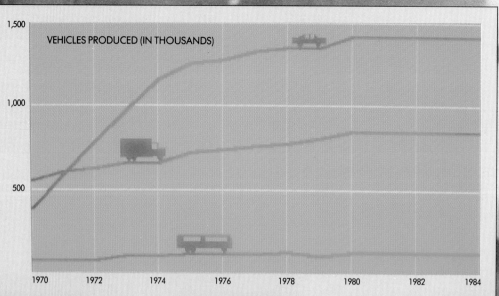

ENTERING THE AUTOMOTIVE AGE

Cars for personal use held low priority in the Soviet scheme until the late 1960s, but since then the output of passenger vehicles has quadrupled, far outstripping modest increases in production of trucks and buses.

Spare parts are scarce, however (accessories are so often stolen that most drivers automatically remove the windshield wipers when they park their cars). And use is limited to the city areas, where good roads exist — but the accident level is high because of the number of novice drivers behind the steering wheels.

VEHICLES PRODUCED (IN THOUSANDS)

1,500

1,000

500

1970 1972 1974 1976 1978 1980 1982 1984

Maintenance workers sweep leaves off the median strip of a six-lane highway, the Lenin Prospekt, one of the country's few modern roads. The U.S.S.R.

has just 300,000 miles of paved roads — less than a tenth of the paved mileage of the United States.

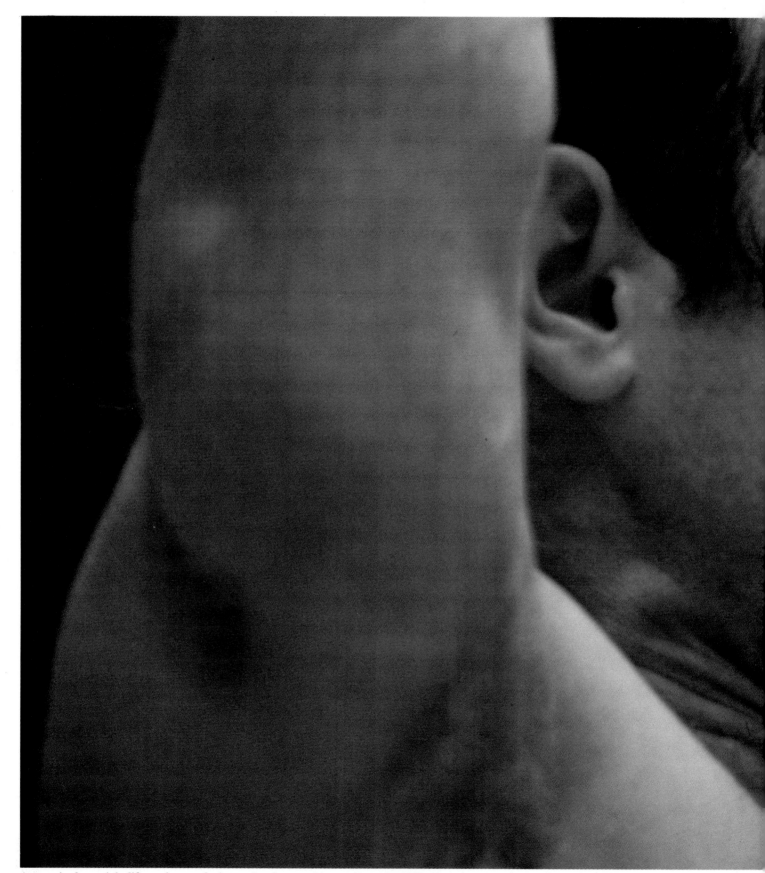

Arms raised, a weight lifter grimaces during national competitions prior to the 1980 Olympic games. In the nine weight-lifting events that year, Soviet

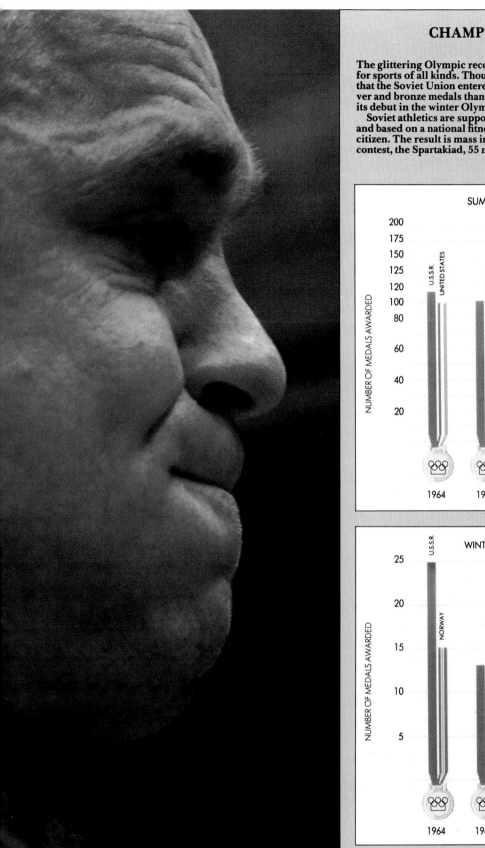

CHAMPIONS OF THE OLYMPICS

The glittering Olympic record of the Soviets indicates the national enthusiasm for sports of all kinds. Though it was not until the summer Olympics of 1952 that the Soviet Union entered the games, Soviet athletes made off with more silver and bronze medals than the United States. And when the U.S.S.R. made its debut in the winter Olympics of 1956, it won the most medals and points.

Soviet athletics are supported by a complex of government organizations and based on a national fitness program that attempts to include almost every citizen. The result is mass involvement in competitions. In one pre-Olympic contest, the Spartakiad, 55 million people took part in 27 events.

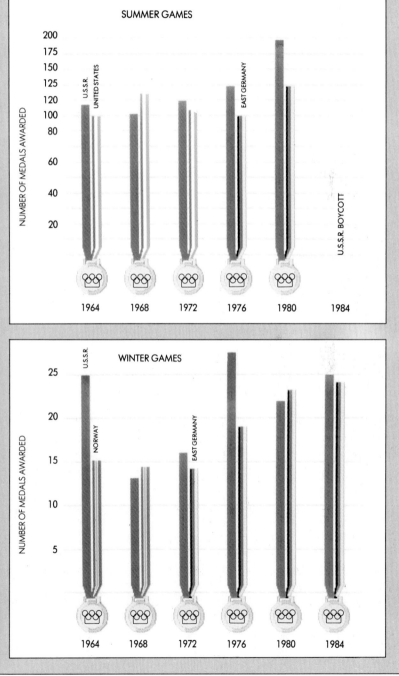

citizens took four gold medals — and athletes from U.S.S.R. satellites won the other five.

Workers on a collective farm in Siberia sit down to lunch near their tractors, the widely used 130-horsepower DT-75M. Despite the harsh climate, the

A CLIMATE TO TRY
THE SPIRIT

A climate map of the Soviet Union corroborates the country's reputation for frigid winters — and helps to account for the difficulties and setbacks of Soviet agriculture.

Only in three small areas — along the Black Sea and near Afghanistan and China — are there long, warm growing seasons. Much of the North is polar tundra; most of the Southeast is chilly and arid; all of the rest has winter temperatures that dip below −36° F. Indeed, so cold does it get that almost all of the Soviet Union's northern coast is never entirely free of ice, and even the southern port of Odessa on the Black Sea is frozen in for six weeks or so each winter. Only the coastal area of the Kola Peninsula in the far northwest does not freeze; this is because the Gulf Stream flows nearby.

LONG SUMMER;
MILD WINTER

ARID STEPPE
OR DESERT

WARM SHORT SUMMER;
SEVERE WINTER

COOL SHORT SUMMER;
SEVERE WINTER

COLD SHORT SUMMER;
SEVERE WINTER

SHORT SUMMER;
MOST SEVERE WINTER

POLAR TUNDRA

acreage cultivated in Soviet Asia has been almost doubled in the past two decades.

MEETING THE CONSUMER'S WANTS

In the decades since the Stalin era, the emphasis in the Soviet economy has shifted somewhat from heavy industry, to bring Soviet consumers more of the tangibles that make modern life pleasant, as indicated by these production figures. The manufacture of radios has doubled; the output of television sets and washing machines has quadrupled; and production of refrigerators has increased 12-fold, though in the early 1980s production leveled off. Statistics for washing machines show a drop between 1970 and 1980 when automatic washers replaced obsolete, so-called semi-automatic models.

For the first time, the Soviet Union's citizens are demanding quality in the appliances they buy. The government now awards a "Seal of Quality" to goods that meet international standards. But of the 42 refrigerator models available in the late 1970s, only five were given the seal, and of the 40 washing machines, just three got it.

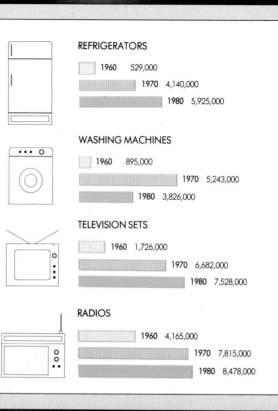

REFRIGERATORS

1960   529,000
1970   4,140,000
1980   5,925,000

WASHING MACHINES

1960   895,000
1970   5,243,000
1980   3,826,000

TELEVISION SETS

1960   1,726,000
1970   6,682,000
1980   7,528,000

RADIOS

1960   4,165,000
1970   7,815,000
1980   8,478,000

Their lighted windows spelling U.S.S.R. in Cyrillic characters, modern offices on Moscow's Kalinin Prospekt house ministries that regulate output of

consumer and industrial goods. This street also has fashionable shops and cafés.

When most people think of the Soviet Union, they conjure up an image of a huge, cold country made up of lonely villages scattered amid dark forests and across open steppe and bleak tundra. The image is only partly accurate. There is no denying the size of the country. A train traveling 1,200 miles a day would take an entire month to go around the perimeter of the U.S.S.R. And villages do indeed abound. Yet the Soviet Union is not rural but urban. Twice as many people live in its cities and towns as in the countryside. There are more than 2,000 cities and towns — and 20 completely new towns mushroom into existence each year. Of the cities, 272 have populations of 100,000 or more, and 23 have more than a million. Moscow, the 800-year-old capital that is called simply "the center," is the largest of these, with 8.2 million inhabitants. Even far off in the Siberian wilds, Novosibirsk has a population of 1.3 million. The urbanization of the country parallels its conversion from an agricultural backwater to an industrial power, a process begun under the Tsars and pressed relentlessly since the Revolution. It has led to remarkable achievement and terrible failure.

The number of people moving from the country to take jobs in the cities is steadily rising: Since 1918, the percentage of population living in cities has more than tripled. The government has never been able to meet the need for housing, a problem exacerbated by the destruction of six million houses and apartment buildings during World War II. A postwar building effort continues unabated, providing two million newly constructed — though small — dwellings each year. To create new housing, 420 plants turn out prefabricated sections *(opposite)*, which are quickly assembled into buildings.

The growth of cities has been accompanied by a corresponding growth in services. Moscow, Leningrad, Kiev, Kharkov, Baku, Yerevan, Tbilisi and Tashkent all have subways, and another eight cities are scheduled to get them. Moscow's Metro, operated by a staff of 22,500, has 127 miles of track and nearly 200 stations to serve seven million passengers daily. The city's buses operate on 1,000 routes and provide 15 million rides a day.

While the cities continue to expand, an effort is being made to regulate their growth, particularly that of Moscow, which has doubled its population since 1939. In 1975, ninety-five industrial plants were moved out of Moscow to reduce congestion and pollution. Current plans call for the diversion of heavy industry to 14 satellite communities that will be constructed around the city before the year 2000. A ring of parkland 30 miles wide is envisaged as a green buffer zone between the satellites and the city proper. Already 40 per cent of Moscow is made up of parks and public gardens, and on the outskirts is the so-called dacha zone of weekend cottages.

Some funds for urban expansion come from taxes, but much of the money is revenue from businesses run by cities. The Moscow municipal administration is one of the world's largest commercial

A prefabricated wall section, complete with windows, is hoisted into place during construction of an apartment building in Khabarovsk, in eastern Siberia. The same standardized parts are used throughout the Soviet Union to speed the completion of badly needed housing.

conglomerates, with almost 1.5 million employees. Nearly all cafés, taxis, bakeries, theaters, retail shops and consumer-goods manufacturers, as well as services such as dry-cleaning and hairdressing establishments and the public transportation system, are owned by the city. It even owns plants that manufacture prefabricated sections for apartment buildings it erects. The income from all these ventures goes into city coffers.

Many of the newest urban centers have arisen where before there were only settlements of log houses—or empty wasteland. Siberia, once a sparsely inhabited realm of endless forests and swamps, is the site of instant cities erected to further the development of that region's numerous resources, and it is here that the problems of rapid growth become most obvious.

At Neryungri, in frigid country only 600 miles from the Arctic Circle, 40,000 people live and work on land that a few years ago was wilderness. Neryungri sits atop one of the world's richest deposits

of coal, which could be converted to coke and taken east by rail for export to Japan. The U.S.S.R. has invested millions of dollars to build the town and dig a huge open-pit mine—all against great odds, including winter cold so bitter that it causes rubber tires to crumble and steel to shatter.

But plan and reality failed to mesh, as they often have in Siberia. The project fell two years behind schedule. Heavy-duty mining equipment imported from Japan and the United States was mishandled, causing chassis underpinnings to crack and hydraulic lines to burst in the cold. The project manager blamed the foreign machinery. But articles in *Pravda* pointed to failures closer to home. Poorly compounded concrete crumbled in the subzero temperatures, slowing construction of the coke-producing plant, a power station and a dam. Moscow's Ministry of Coal Industry failed to authorize covered workshops for the costly machines before they went into operation; servicing and repairs had to be done in the open even in winter. The Ministry neglected to order spare parts. One giant power shovel stood idle a whole year, said *Pravda*, while the mine management "bombarded the Ministry with telegrams asking for the spare parts, to no avail." Meanwhile, the world economy changed, clouding the prospect of profitable exports to Japan. To a Western correspondent who visited troubled Neryungri, the complex seemed likely to "become a monument to the ills of the Soviet economy—impressive in scale, but consuming vast amounts of capital that its revenue may never repay."

17

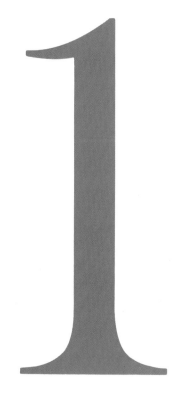

Primping while they watch strollers,
two young women relax on a
Moscow park bench on their weekend.

18

THE GOOD LIFE

Downtown Moscow's main subway line stops at Dzerzhinsky Square, a broad plaza of sedate prerevolutionary buildings that include, among others, the headquarters of the KGB, the Committee for State Security. Few people among the soberly clad multitudes that swarm out of the trains give it much notice, however. They turn instead, shopping bags in hand, to one of the square's large department stores, Children's World, the Soviet Union's grandest emporium for skates, baby carriages, volleyballs and dolls.

Inside its doors, long lines of customers press in upon the sales counters. In one line, a woman visitor from Tbilisi, a city some 1,200 miles to the south, stands to buy a pair of children's long winter underwear — a commodity that is in short supply at home. In another line, for sleds, the wait is six hours. But the sleds are there; a few years earlier, they were not.

The same scene is acted out daily at GUM department store, one of Moscow's largest, four blocks south on Red Square, opposite the Kremlin. Shoppers queue for shaving cream from East Germany and toothpaste from Bulgaria, for cheeses and salamis and rare smoked sturgeon, for radios and refrigerators, for sweaters from Poland or dresses from Finland. At a necktie display that includes a poster explaining how to tie a cravat, a young man copies down hints; he is about to purchase his first tie. Probably neither his peasant grandfather nor his father ever wore one. All across the Union of Soviet Socialist Republics, from Kalin-

ingrad in the West to Vladivostok in the East, the 278 million inhabitants of the world's first Communist state are elbowing their way toward their share of the consumer goods that in recent decades began coming to market in quantity.

The supply of consumer goods is one measure of the way the diverse peoples of this, the largest of all countries, live today, after centuries of poverty, invasion and oppression. Most Soviet citizens are reasonably well off, though not as much so as their counterparts in, say, France or Japan. Not only are there sufficient food, shelter and warm (if not always stylish) clothing, but such luxuries as the imported sweaters and shaving cream are obtainable.

Almost every adult — male and female — has a job, vacations, leisure time and a wide variety of activities to enjoy, ranging from theatergoing to mountain climbing. Children are lavished with affection, jealously protected, and educated (as well as indoctrinated) in a massive school system. The state regulates almost every aspect of life, yet intermittently tolerates, then cracks down on, independent activity — even including a counterculture, of sorts. A generation ago life in this country was different.

A Moscow grandmother, remembering the 1940s, describes the living conditions of a family she knew — a near-illiterate husband, an overburdened and sickly wife, and 11 children. "All lived in one big, big room — in a barracks, really," with several other families. "They had a curtain which

they pulled across it, and they put the beds behind the curtain. They used to sleep in shifts."

Today, she explains, "the children are all grown up, and married, and have their own children. Each has an apartment. Small. One or two rooms. But with conveniences — a stove, maybe a refrigerator. One has a car. They simply can't imagine that life could be any better."

Most others in the Soviet Union would agree. Over the past quarter century, food consumption has doubled, from bare sustenance to 3,300 calories per person each day. This is nearly the French average, although much of it is made up of potatoes and bread. Real incomes have quadrupled, the work week has been shortened from six days to five, and day-to-day consumer spending has gone up threefold. Three quarters of all Russian families own refrigerators, two thirds have washing machines, and 22 per cent have vacuum cleaners. And almost all now own television sets — 25 per cent of which are color sets. But only one out of 15 has a telephone.

To be sure, there are flaws in this rosy picture. Prices have risen for everything but staples. In the early 1980s, milk, butter and certain other basics had to be rationed in some areas because of poor harvests, and the quality of food declined: Chickens were scrawny and the butterfat content of milk dropped from 3.6 to 2.2 per cent (half that of Danish milk). A new bitter edge consequently appeared on the national sense of humor. In one jest, a Russian and a visiting Westerner hear of a Communist Party decree that there will be no queues for sausage.

"What is a queue?" the visitor asks the Russian.

"What is a sausage?" responds his Soviet friend.

The best goods are reserved for the elite, including top Communist Party members and favored artists, writers and scientists, among others. The grandmother's car-owning friend belongs to the fortunate 6 per cent who have been able to make such a purchase, and he had to wait perhaps five years on a government list to reserve the chance to do so.

Queues, though fewer, are still a familiar nuisance; when poet Andrei Voznesensky gives a recital at Moscow's Writer's Club, he brings down the house with his enumeration of his place in a list of lines, beginning with one for a famous ballerina's performance and ending with one for a new car:

I am 41st for Plisetskaya,
33rd for the theater at Taganka,
45th for the graveyard at Vagankovo.
I am 14th for the eye specialist,
21st for Glazunov, the artist,
45th for an abortion
(When my turn comes, I'll be in shape),
I am 103rd for auto parts
(They signed me up when I was born),
I am 10,007th for a new car
(They signed me up before I was born).

To a considerable extent these complaints result from rising expectations, especially among the young, who never knew the bad old days of Stalin or the Tsar. Yet there are also signs of a real and disquieting decline in the quality of Soviet life. They show up in two key indicators that are thought to reflect a people's nutrition and medical care: infant mortality and life expectancy.

Until the late 1970s, the Soviet Union, like nearly all nations, reported these statistics regularly. Then publication of the nationwide figures stopped, itself a portentous event. However, scattered local figures continued to appear, and they have been compiled by Murray Feshbach, a research scholar at Georgetown University in Washington, D.C. His compilations, widely accepted as accurate, indicate that life expectancy for men dropped from a high of 66 years in 1965-1966 to 61.9 in the early 1980s (compared with Sweden's 72.8). Meanwhile infant mortality climbed from 22.9 per 1,000 births in 1971 to 28 to 30 per 1,000 in 1980 (compared with Sweden's 6.9 in 1980).

This mixed picture of a good life

RUSSIA'S CYRILLIC ALPHABET

The listing below of the Soviet Union's Cyrillic alphabet includes a guide to pronunciation and to the transliterations employed in this volume. The alphabet was named for Saint Cyril, a Greek missionary who helped convert Slavs to Christianity in the Ninth Century. It was originally derived from the Greek alphabet by Saint Cyril and his brother, Saint Methodius, also an early Christian missionary.

CYRILLIC	TRANSLITERATION	PRONUNCIATION	CYRILLIC	TRANSLITERATION	PRONUNCIATION
А	a	as in father	Р	r	as in ravioli (rolled r)
Б	b	as in bit	С	s	as in Soviet
В	v	as in vote	Т	t	as in ten
Г	g	as in goat	У	u	as in pool
Д	d	as in dog	Ф	f	as in fit
Е	e	as in yes or as in machine	Х	kh	as in Bach in German
Ё	e	as in yoke	Ц	ts	as in cats
Ж	zh	as in azure	Ч	ch	as in cheer
З	z	as in zero	Ш	sh	as in shop
И	i	as in machine	Щ	shch	as in fresh sheets
Й	i	as in boy	Ъ		hard sign, no pronunciation
К	k	as in kit			
Л	l	as in let	Ы	y	as in shrill
М	m	as in map	Ь		soft sign, no pronunciation
Н	n	as in not			
О	o	as in note or as in father	Э	e	as in bed
П	p	as in pat	Ю	iu	as in cute
			Я	ia	as in yacht

marred by serious failures comes clearer in close examination of individuals. The intimate details of their homes and families tell much about life in the Soviet Union in the latter part of the 20th Century.

Two thirds of the Soviet people live west of the Ural Mountains in Europe, and 60 per cent are city-dwellers. Most of these urbanites are the children and grandchildren of peasants who left farm villages for such centers as Moscow, Leningrad, Kiev, Kharkov and Gorky in search of a better life.

For the offspring of peasants, the Revolution has paid off. Virtually all are literate, and many hold university degrees admitting them to a burgeoning middle class of doctors, teachers and engineers — the so-called intelligentsia, those who work with their heads rather than their hands. It is toward this group of middle-level professionals that the rewards of Soviet progress promise to flow most bounteously — and among whom the battle to secure them is most intense.

Charter members of this new middle class are Dmitri and Sofia Ivanov. (These are not their real names, nor are most others in this book; the Soviet government does not look kindly on citizens who discuss their personal lives with foreigners.) The Ivanovs live in a 12-story apartment house in the Ukrainian city of Kiev. They share an apartment with their son and daughter-in-law, who are saving for a place of their own. Sofia's father was exiled to Siberia before the Revolution for being a Bolshevik, and later became headmaster of a school there. Dmitri's father grew up in a tiny log house, its only amenity a wood-burning brick stove for baking bread and cooking the cabbage soup, beets and potatoes that sustained the family. He volunteered for a Siberian "new lands" project in the 1930s, became a party member, and later worked as the director of a dairy.

Like virtually all Soviet citizens, Dmitri and Sofia work for the government — he as a mechanical engineer for the railroad, she as an art teacher at a Kiev high school. Dmitri earns 330 rubles a month — nearly double the 180-ruble average salary because his party membership ensures him a good position — while Sofia earns 150 rubles. Their son gets 110 rubles from his job and his wife another 110 rubles. The family's living costs are low because many necessities are subsidized by the state. They pay only 20 rubles a month in rent — the apartment is owned by Dmitri's employer. Party dues are three per cent of their salary, income tax just 7 per cent. The monthly grocery bill for the four comes to 230 rubles, thanks to subsidized staples such as bread, milk and sugar. Meat and fresh vegetables are more expensive because they are bought on the free farmers' market, were quality is better but prices reflect supply and demand.

The Ivanovs' apartment, in a new section of Kiev, is one of millions built in recent decades. It offers unpretentious comfort: two small rooms for both living and sleeping, an eat-in kitchen, a hallway, a bathroom and a separate cubicle for the toilet. There is also a small balcony that in winter takes overflow from the tiny refrigerator and in summer holds pots of flowers.

The Ivanovs have furnished the apartment with an eye toward dual function. Sofas double as beds at night, a worktable becomes a dinner table when guests arrive. One room displays a wall of books — a prominent feature in the home of any educated family — and a black-and-white television set. The floors are bare polished wood. (Rugs are so uncommon in the Soviet Union that when an obscure Moscow store announced it would take orders for delivery the following year, a crowd of 10,000 to 15,000 people lined up overnight to sign up.)

The overall effect of the Ivanovs' apartment is similar to that of middle-class homes elsewhere in Eastern Europe. Scant personality emerges.

1

("When I die," complains one Soviet woman, "no one will know what kind of taste I had. All my life I have bought what was available, not what I wanted.")

In the bathroom the Ivanovs have installed a washing machine; it cleans the laundry but does not rinse it or spin it dry. The water must be changed and each garment wrung out by hand, then hung to dry on the balcony. The hot water comes from a gas-fired heater that the Ivanovs bought; their building, like most, supplies only cold water.

Although the Ivanovs are proud of their apartment, they complain about its lack of space. Back in the 1920s the government decreed that each Soviet citizen was to be allotted 98 square feet of living quarters (excluding kitchen and bath), the equivalent of a room 10 feet square. But this goal has been reached in only a few of the large cities. Through the Stalin years, city-dwellers, like the family described by the grandmother, crowded into subdivided communal apartments holding as many as 60 people. A family of four was lucky to have a room to itself, while kitchen, bathroom and utilities had to be shared with other tenants. Even in Moscow and Leningrad, people still lived in wood cottages with outdoor plumbing.

In the late 1950s, Nikita Khrushchev launched a massive building program. Thousands upon thousands of five-story walkups mushroomed. So hurriedly were the buildings put up that they began falling apart almost as soon as the mortar dried. On some, wire-mesh screens have been fitted like awnings to catch bricks that tumble down from façades above. People refer to these structures as *khrushchobi,* a derisive pun that joins the late Premier's name with the word for "slum."

The *khrushchobi* are gradually being

superseded by slablike nine- to 12-story high rises similar to the Ivanovs', assembled from prefabricated concrete panels and identical in design from Minsk to Moscow to Samarkand. Four out of five new structures are built this way, reducing labor costs as much as 40 per cent and shortening construction time from two or three years to as little as three months.

Construction is less sloppy than in the 1950s buildings, but new tenants may still find themselves varnishing floors, painting walls and installing util-

A newly purchased puppy snuggles in its owner's fur coat while payment is made at the *ptichii rynok,* Moscow's thriving pet market.

ities that the builders left unfinished.

Most of the new apartments are grouped in satellite districts on city outskirts. Although the plans call for food markets and schools close by, this is not always the reality, and department stores and theaters — as well as the offices and factories where most residents work — are likely to be an hour or so away, by bus and subway.

Although the new apartments go up at the rate of two million a year, the end is nowhere in sight. One fifth of all city-dwellers are still packed into the old communal flats, where they must argue over their share of the light bill and who gets to cook dinner when. And so a private apartment, even an unfinished one located inconveniently on the edge of town, is a passionately sought goal for which competition is intense.

Nowhere is living space more desirable than in the Soviet capital. There is a saying that "Moscow is downhill from all the Russias" — the good things in life tend to flow there first. But before anyone can move to Moscow to share them, he or she must first obtain a residency permit. And they are not easy to get: Only a job or marriage to a Muscovite guarantees that the move will be permitted. Marriages of convenience may be contracted with Moscow residents who are total strangers. Vows are spoken, the place of residence is changed on the interior passport everyone must carry, then money passes under the table and there is a quick divorce.

But a residency permit is only half the battle. Nobel Prize-winning physicist Peter Kapitsa told the story of how his cleaning woman managed to acquire her own flat during the Khrushchev era. Kapitsa, then working on a secret project, was given a direct telephone line from his home to Premier

Nikolai Bulganin. Early one morning the cleaning woman picked up the receiver, roused Bulganin from sleep, and laid out her problem. The next day the special telephone was removed but the cleaning woman got her apartment.

High-level influence remains the best avenue to all such perquisites, but most people must use humbler means. One method is to join the street-corner bargaining at one of the city's unofficial housing exchanges. Here crowds of apartment seekers mill about with placards announcing what they need and what they can swap for it. (Once a citizen obtains an apartment from government authorities, it becomes a small fiefdom that can be traded, rented or even bequeathed to children.)

In a typical exchange, an older couple with a newlywed daughter offers to exchange a four-room flat for two separate units, one for each family. Also looking for a swap are a young painter and his wife trying to parlay their two rooms into three in order to make room for their second child. As leverage, the painter has persuaded his parents to include their four-room apartment in the deal. He wants to exchange his apartment and his parents' for two three-room apartments. Finally, after weeks of negotiation, an agreement is struck and six apartments change hands in a transaction involving eight families.

In part because housing is so tight, urban families tend to be small among the ethnic Russians, who make up a bare majority of the population. Many couples limit themselves to a single child. Birth-control means are limited, but abortions are easily available (some women have undergone more than a dozen). As a result the birth rate among ethnic Russians is one of the world's lowest, about 16 births for every 1,000 individuals. To reverse the trend, the government imposes a 10 per cent income-tax penalty on childless couples. Even so, those who choose to avoid parenthood come out ahead financially. Typically, the money they save is poured into their home.

One such childless couple are Anna and Volodya, two Moscow friends of an American exchange student and his wife. Anna is a handsome strawberry blonde in her late 30s who works as a supervisor in a paint factory. Volodya, her husband, is a tall, balding industrial technician in his 40s, grown pudgy from lack of exercise and too many boiled potatoes.

Anna and Volodya live in a three-room apartment that they share with Volodya's grandmother, an ancient peasant woman with a merry, wrinkled face and a bun of thinning gray hair. The apartment is furnished modestly except for a West German stereo, their proudest possession, which was purchased at great expense on the black market, along with a large collection of black-market records. Frank Sinatra and Ray Charles are the favorites.

As in most Russian families, the good life, for Anna and Volodya, begins at home and centers on the kitchen table. "Everything is better at home," says Volodya. "Moscow stores are crowded, the metro and buses are jungles, restaurants are impossible to get into."

So it is around the kitchen table that couples like Anna and Volodya entertain. Food appears in no particular order, and family and friends jostle one another, elbow to elbow. Swept away by the intensities of Russian friendship, they linger for hours, indulging in talk that runs from trivialities to cosmic issues of God and humanity.

Sometimes the meal is no more than

"Bruins Play Hockey" is the prize attraction of the Moscow Ice Circus, one of more than 80 troupes — with a total of 6,000 performers and 14,000 offstage workers — that make up the Soviet national circus.

a clear soup with some fragrant black bread, or perhaps a mound of boiled potatoes and some pickled mushrooms — all washed down with glasses of sweet black tea or iced vodka. But at Anna's table, meals are more likely to take on another dimension.

Sunday lunch might begin with cabbage borscht or sorrel-and-kidney soup, followed by fresh tomatoes and cucumbers in sour cream, four kinds of bread, potatoes drenched in butter, beef or duck swimming in gravy, then fried cheese cakes with homemade plum jam and a cream-filled torte from a bakery. There may be wine from Georgia, cognac from Armenia or flavored vodkas.

Maintaining this life style requires unflagging effort from both Anna and Volodya. Like many people in other societies, they find that their regular paychecks do not cover the comforts and luxuries they insist on having. "If you really get mad at another person," one Russian explains, "you put a curse on him: 'Let him live on his salary.' It's a terrible fate."

And so Volodya moonlights. He is a skillful photographer, and he has found an underground source for East German color film, which is far better than Russian film. He uses it to photograph children, going around to the elementary schools in Moscow and buying the principals' cooperation with bottles of Armenian cognac. Then he sells the photographs to the children's parents. "It's a very nice arrangement," he says. "The principal gets his cognac, the parents get pictures of their darlings that are much better than the black-and-white junk. And I, of course, make a profit."

Although freelance enterprises of this type are officially frowned on, millions of people engage in them. Such transactions are often the only way to obtain prized goods and services. Even a haircut is easier to get if the customer goes to the barber's home, after hours, and pays a little extra to avoid the long waits at the government barber shop.

Among the chief practitioners of under-the-counter operations are salespeople in government stores, who hold back merchandise for special cus-

tomers. The humor magazine *Krokodil* frequently lampoons this practice. In one issue it mimicked a store's public-address announcement of the arrival of new merchandise: "Dear customer, in the leather goods department a shipment of 500 imported women's purses has been received. Four hundred and fifty of them have been bought by employees of the store. Forty-nine have

been ordered in advance by friends. One purse is in the display window. We invite you to visit the leather department and buy this purse."

As the *Krokodil* satire indicates, this thriving underground trade depends more on favoritism than on outright bribery. People trade their own special advantages for those of others. Irina, the wife of a Leningrad musician who works for the Kirov ballet and opera, can always get tickets for a few of the seats set aside for high party officials and visiting dignitaries. Some she gives to a friend who is a surgeon at a large hospital, and in return the surgeon makes sure that Irina's family receives preferential treatment. The uneven quality of Soviet health care makes this good insurance.

Irina also passes on tickets to her hairdresser, or to a dressmaker who copies Paris styles from magazines that Irina borrows from her sister — who works for Intourist and has access to Western periodicals. So Irina stays *à la mode* and the dressmaker sees the ballet.

This elaborate system of barter and favor-swapping is so pervasive partly because bureaucratic bumbling causes periodic shortages, partly because scarce imported goods are preferred over shoddy Soviet products. By the government's own admission, only 1.4 per cent of its consumer goods measure up to international standards. Factory-made clothes come unstitched after several wearings, and shoes are so poor that in a recent year one pair out of eight had to be rejected by the official shoe inspectors.

Mechanical products are notoriously unreliable. The country's best slide projector has to be turned off every 20 minutes to keep it from overheating. Even dress snaps do not always work.

1

In a letter to the magazine *Krest'ianka (Peasant Woman)*, one exasperated woman complained of buying "quality" snaps that, while attractive, were nearly impossible to close. "I tried my hands, teeth, even a hammer — nothing doing," she wrote. "Then I had a happy thought — pliers! Since then, I go nowhere without pliers."

Under-the-counter sales are also spurred by the inept distribution system, which causes sporadic shortages in mundane items. Months may go by when it is impossible to buy detergent, or toothpaste or frying pans. In Alma-Ata recently, the stores ran out of ballpoint pens. One man recalls spending weeks looking for a push broom; there were plenty of brush heads, he said, but none had handles. Yet a few months earlier the stores were carrying the handles without the brushes.

Shopping can be a challenge not only because of shortages but also because of the way retail stores operate. To buy food for Anna and Volodya's Sunday lunch, Anna first must line up to select the item — a pound of cheese, for example — and determine its price. Then she must join another line to pay a cashier and get a receipt. Finally, she lines up a third time with her receipt, to pick up her purchase.

At each store she is shoved and jostled by other customers and is confronted by surly sales clerks. Soviet salespeople, who may be deeply warm and generous at home and with their friends, put on their rudest manners when dealing with the public.

Waiting in line is such a basic and unavoidable part of daily life that it becomes a job in itself. The average urban Soviet woman spends 14 hours a week queuing up — two hours each day. The Soviet press once reported that 30 bil-

lion woman-hours a year are spent in this manner.

Almost every time she leaves home, a Soviet woman carries with her a string bag, an *avos'ka* — for "just in case." Along her route, she looks for targets of opportunity. Whenever she sees a line forming, she rushes to join it, often before knowing what is being offered. If the goods hold out and she holds onto her place, she may be able to stuff her *avos'ka* with a woolen shawl or a pair of Italian shoes. More than likely she will also buy extra shawls or shoes, for relatives and friends. People know by heart the clothing sizes of brothers, sisters, parents and co-workers. In every factory and office, workers regularly slip away — despite periodic crackdowns — to prowl the neighborhood in search of desirable buys, and to return laden with goods for distribution or resale to their fellows.

Men take on some of the shopping and queuing chores, but most of the burden falls on women. In their efforts to bring the good life home, women are the unsung heroines of Soviet society. Housework, Lenin once remarked, is "barbarously unproductive, petty, nerve-racking, stultifying and crushing." This condemnation does not prevent modern Soviet males from leaving the job to women. The men neither cook, nor wash dishes, nor change diapers, nor mop the floor. When they arrive home from work, they simply settle down with the newspaper or in front of the television, and wait for their wives to make dinner.

Although the men seldom help at home, most women help outside the home. They are the backbone of the Soviet economy, making up slightly more than half the work force. Some 65 or 70 million — about 85 per cent of all women between the ages of 16 and 54 — hold regular jobs, the highest percentage in any industrialized nation. One third of the U.S.S.R.'s lower-court judges and 70 per cent of its doctors are women. There are more female engineers in the Soviet Union than in all the rest of the world.

Yet, even in the work force, women are second-class citizens, relegated to inferior positions. Many Soviet women who are called physicians or engineers have jobs that elsewhere are filled by technicians. The medical specialists, university professors and prestigious academy members are nearly all men.

As in other countries, most working women hold low-paying teaching and clerical jobs. While they receive the same pay as men for the same work, their average salary is a third less than that of men. But here some even serve as manual laborers. Western visitors never fail to be astonished that Moscow's streets are cleaned by platoons of babushkas with brooms, and that potholes are filled by women construction workers wielding picks and shovels. One Soviet joke calls women "not only the equal of men but also of tractors and bulldozers."

Of the 15 per cent of Russian women who do not hold down regular jobs, some are young mothers. Others are the privileged wives of scientists, athletes, military brass and Communist Party elite. Still others belong to a shadowy fringe of avant-garde painters and poets who somehow manage to get by outside the official economy.

Rima is one such dropout. In her mid-30s, half Georgian and one quarter Jewish, she is a sometime poet who makes her way in the effervescent underground art world of Moscow.

Rima has a friend who holds exhibits in her large apartment, and Rima helps to set them up — preparing canapes, greeting guests, acting as a second hostess. Many of the guests are foreign diplomats and journalists anxious to make contact with Russian intellectuals, and Rima helps to smooth the way. A newly arrived cultural attaché may need language lessons, and she will arrange for them — or give them herself. She will also arrange for the black-market exchange of dollars for rubles, taking a small cut. Or she will earn a commission on the sale of a painting by an artist she is championing.

Rima's catch-as-catch-can income helps support two households. For the record, she lives with her parents in a large apartment that also houses her daughter Natasha and her ex-husband Borya, an ill-paid translator with pretensions as a poet. "Of course I would prefer not to see Borya," she says, "but we Russians can't afford to be emotional that way." The housing shortage prevents Borya from moving out.

Each morning Rima cooks everyone's breakfast, dresses her daughter for school, cleans, shops for dinner, and then embarks on her frenzied round of cross-cultural dealings. In the evening she returns, fixes dinner, helps Natasha with her homework and perhaps washes Borya's shirts. Then she

Indulging a traditional penchant for hard drink, two Soviet citizens prepare to down a newly purchased bottle of vodka in the street. The average adult drinks about 9 liters of distilled spirits annually, more than is consumed in any other country.

27

takes a 40-minute taxi ride across town to her second household. Rima's fiancé lives there, 19-year-old Vasya, another would-be poet who has dropped out of mainstream society.

Vasya shares a tiny ground-floor apartment with several roommates, and Rima prepares dinner for all of them — her second of the day. Her time with her husband-to-be is brief but intense, filled with jealousies brought on by Vasya's resentment of Rima's former spouse. "What can I do?" she shrugs. "Vasya and Borya both have talent, poor things, and someone has to help them."

For Rima, staging parties and filling in as a hostess are paying jobs. For most Soviet women, entertaining at home is the main social activity — a generous spread of food and drink on the kitchen table like that laid on for Sunday lunch by Anna and Volodya. Most leisure time is spent at home, with friends and relatives, reading or watching television, although many attractions also draw people outside during their free time.

Reading is a national habit. In a country where literacy has increased from the prerevolutionary 25 per cent to nearly 99 per cent, Soviet men spend almost an eighth of their free time over a book or newspaper, while women devote a sixth of theirs to this activity. The most popular book topics, as shown by a recent survey of library borrowings, are biography, travel, spy and adventure stories, and — to an astonishing degree — World War II. The memory of that struggle compels an anguished fascination.

Pravda and *Izvestia,* the two main mass-circulation daily newspapers, command readerships of many millions. Both are heavy with political news and party affairs. But there are at least five other specialized papers with circulations in the millions. *Komsomol'skaya pravda* is for members of Komsomol, the Young Communist League, *Sel'skaya zhizn' (Rural Life)* is for country people, *Trud (Labor)* for trade-union members, *Krasnaya zvezda (Red Star)* for the military, and *Literaturnaya gazeta (Literary Gazette)* for the intelligentsia.

Magazines are plentiful and cheap and equally varied in their appeal. They range from the authoritative *Kommunist,* which publishes articles by Soviet leaders, to *Novy mir (New World),* a literary monthly, *Ogonyek (Little Light),* a weekly picture magazine, and the satirical *Krokodil.* In addition to these Russian-language periodicals are numerous regional publications in local languages such as Ukrainian, Estonian and Tadzhik, as well as a host of technical and scientific journals at professional and popular levels.

Then there is television. Men watch several hours a day, twice as much as women. There are four main channels, two of which are beamed from Moscow

to the hinterlands by satellite. The outlying districts, in turn, have their own local stations. Programing varies. For European Soviets, there is an educational channel that emphasizes science. And sports, concerts, ballet and opera get saturation coverage on a special nationwide sports and cultural channel. One of the most popular programs is the *Film Travel Club,* which takes viewers to locations as diverse as Australia's Outback, Brazil's Amazon and the United States' Grand Canyon. It provides a rare window on the world for people who are seldom allowed to venture outside their native land.

On a more intellectual level is the quintessentially Russian pastime of chess. There are some three million ranked chess players in the U.S.S.R., including 50 grand masters, compared with 35 in Yugoslavia, a chess-loving nation second only to the Soviet Union, and 22 in the third-ranking country, the United States. And on summer evenings and weekends, countless devotees gather around the permanent chess tables in city parks to play or to cheer on local champions.

Away from home, an evening out may on special occasions — a wedding or anniversary — include a restaurant meal or a stage performance. But most often the excursion is to a movie.

The Soviet Union has more than half of all the motion-picture theaters in the world, and they sell about 80 million tickets a week (at an average price of 50 cents). They show some foreign films — heavily censored not only for political content but also for eroticism — but mainly domestic productions. Some 150 features in several languages are produced each year in 40 studios in Moscow and other cities. Many of these movies are of very high

A woman steps up to be weighed on one of the scales, tended by pensioners, that are a feature in parks.

28

quality — well acted, artistically staged and expertly photographed. The Communist regime early singled out motion pictures as an art form to be cultivated, and the influential work of prominent Russian directors of the 1920s — Sergei Eisenstein, Vsevolod Pudovkin and Alexander Dovzhenko — has been carried forward by modern film makers.

When not attending movies, most people indulge a passion for athletics and nature. Sports facilities — fields for soccer and volleyball, basketball courts, large indoor swimming pools — are provided by factories and municipalities. In winter, families go ice skating in city parks, and in winter or summer they head by car or *elektrichka* — electric commuter train — for the farmlands and forests that rim the large cities. On such a *vykhodnoi* — going-out day — there may be picnics, mushroom hunting or cross-country skiing. For some, the destination is a dacha, literally a "country villa," although most dachas are not so grand. They tend to be little wooden cottages without water or electricity. Some are privately owned; others are government rewards. Often they can be rented by weekenders.

For the great majority who have no dachas, there are state-controlled resorts on the warm southern beaches of the Black Sea. Each summer the town of Sochi alone is host to some two million Soviets who come there to vacation at government health spas on passes handed out by their unions.

Such passes entitle the recipient to a three- to five-week stay, with almost 90 per cent of the bill paid by the employer. For this, the vacationer gets a bed, meals, mud baths, sunbathing and an organized routine. At one of these rest homes near Odessa, the schedule is: reveille at 7 a.m., half an hour of gymnastics before breakfast (served in two shifts), medical checkups and treatment, sports, an after-lunch siesta, cultural programs, recommended readings and sunbathing that is carefully monitored to prevent overexposure.

Most holidaymakers enjoy this routine. The major drawback to the employer-subsidized vacation is its separation of families. Husband and wife must often vacation apart because they work for different employers. Conse-

quently, many families prefer to go south on their own and rent accommodations in the apartment of a local resident. In most cities a government bureau helps find lodgings, promoting a lucrative free-enterprise tourist trade.

Aside from this summertime fling in the sun, Soviet citizens find warmth all year round in the *bania*. Every hamlet and collective has one of these steam baths, where customers thrash their own — or each others' — sweating bodies with sheaves of aromatic birch twigs to cleanse the dirt from their pores and the day's ills from their souls.

The most famous *bania* is Moscow's Sandunovsky Baths, a lavishly ornate structure from tsarist times, with ancient, much-darned flowered carpets, lace-shaded lamps and molding of plaster cupids. There is one bath for men and another for women, and a visit entails a well-established ritual.

A bather enters the dressing room and exchanges street clothes for a toga-like sheet, then walks into a steam room where the heat takes the breath away. In the women's bath birch-slapping is frowned on. But men flail away with the leafy bundles.

"Simply waving the birch switches caused the air to circulate and increased the heat," wrote one foreign visitor. "We struck each other with the birches and pressed their hot wet leaves against our legs and arms and stomachs so that the heat burrowed beneath the skin and into the vitals. Sweat began to pour and soon the tips of my toes, the last to warm, felt the heat." There followed a plunge into an icy pool.

In the women's baths, the pool scene is one of unfettered freedom. "The water around us was full of women playing tag, shrieking and ducking each other, paddling across the pool," re-

1

ports a young American woman. "The pool itself was elegant, tiled in a mosaic design of garlands. In a niche at one end stood a gold statue of two cherubs, one attempting a half-nelson on the other. With their bulging bodies and homemade knitted bathing caps, the splashing women looked a little incongruous in this setting."

After the pool comes the scrubbing room, where, on long marble slabs lined up like hospital beds, bodies are scoured with handfuls of fresh white-pine shavings until the skin is pink and tender. A quick rinse with buckets of cool water concludes the scrubbing, and the whole procedure begins again with another session in the inferno.

It is between bouts of steaming and scrubbing, however, that the main business of the *bania* takes place. Lounging in the paneled and upholstered dressing rooms, the regulars meet with their friends. Here, over plates of dried salt fish (eaten to replace the salt lost through sweating) and glasses of ice-cold vodka or beer, they joke and talk of their jobs, of troubles with boyfriends or girlfriends, of last night's soccer game or concert or the latest book. The *bania* is everyone's private club.

In the *bania*, at home around the kitchen table, at picnics or soccer games, the one constant ingredient of every social gathering is vodka. In the Muslim areas of Central Asia, religion forbids the use of alcohol, but in European Russia and in Siberia every man drinks, and many women do too — both in quantities that astonish Westerners.

The consumption of distilled spirits per citizen 15 years old or older is 9.4 liters a year. This rate is the highest in the world, followed by Poland, where the average is 5.4 liters. Sales of vodka in the Soviet Union have risen fivefold

since World War II. This figure covers only the vodka that is sold under government supervision. It omits the illegal brew, *samogon,* distilled in large quantities in the countryside.

Contributing to this prodigious consumption is the Russian practice of gulping rather than sipping. Any festivity is punctuated by multiple toasts tossed back neat. The very packaging adds to the problem; the vodka bottle is sealed by a strip of metal foil but no stopper. Once opened, it will probably be emptied on the spot. Outside any factory at closing time can be seen small groups of men tippling away in a rite called "three on a bottle." It takes about 10 minutes to empty a half-liter bottle.

Alcoholism plagues every level of society. It has been blamed for inefficiency at work, absenteeism and crime. More than 50,000 men died of acute alcohol poisoning in 1980 alone — three times as many per capita as in neighboring Finland, where alcohol consumption also runs high.

Women, too, are drinking more. Alcoholism has been cited as "female illness No. 3" in the Soviet Union, after cancer and heart disease. In half the divorce cases drunkenness is given as the reason. Not even a 300 per cent hike in the price of a liter of vodka seems to have had a moderating effect.

In 1985 new Soviet General Secretary Mikhail Gorbachev wasted no time in assigning a high priority to the eradication of alcoholism; raising the drinking age and delaying the opening hours for liquor stores were among the first steps announced by the government.

This rampant alcoholism is seen by many as symptomatic of a declining quality of Soviet life. But there is one element in their lives that offers the Soviet people hope: their children. "We

save the best for the children," they say. "They are our future."

For Elena, a language instructor at Moscow University, life's greatest pleasure is her two-year-old son, Sasha. Hour after hour she dandles him on her knee, cuddling, cooing and singing nursery rhymes, kissing him on the face and mouth, stuffing him with candy so that he stays butterball plump. In winter, before taking him outside, she swaddles him in layer upon layer of clothing — woolen tights, tunic, several oversized sweaters, scarves, felt boots, fur coat and hat — the bundling that turns Russian children, in one observer's eyes, into "walking cabbages."

Like most Soviet mothers, Elena will smother Sasha with love and protection almost up to his teens — feeding him too much, hovering over him as he plays and studies. "I want ten more like him," she says, although the housing shortage will probably limit her to Sasha and one other.

Pampered and spoiled, their every wish catered to, Soviet children are almost never punished or even scolded at home. Yet they grow up disciplined and obedient to authority. They are indoctrinated with the need to conform, to subjugate individual desires to the aims of the group, not only in school, but also in the political organizations to which they belong — the Children of October for youngsters seven to nine and the Young Pioneers for those between 10 and 15. To be honored for meeting the standards of the group is the highest commendation; to be humiliated for disgracing the group is the worst reprimand. And it is often the child's playmates and schoolmates — not parents or teachers — who apply this pressure for conformity.

The first lesson in conformity arrives

A vase of flowers brightens a modest Palace of Weddings as a bride and groom listen to the ceremony. The proceedings are not long; a Palace may hold 50 weddings on a busy Saturday.

THE SOCIALIST RITE OF MARRIAGE

In the secular Soviet Union, the state makes a brave attempt to endow weddings with official, rather than religious, ceremony. Legal registration of the marriage is required, as in most countries, but it usually takes place in a Palace of Weddings *(left)* rather than a plain government office. And it is embroidered with time-honored customs: an exchange of rings, a sermon on the commitment marriage entails, and a nuptial kiss. The state also encourages another "socialist rite," a visit to a monument or shrine *(left, below)*.

After these ceremonies, traditional conviviality takes over. A city-dwelling family may spend six months' pay on a wedding party. In the countryside, vodka-fueled celebrations may last three days. The state even gives encouragement to this feasting; the parents can receive as much as 10 days' leave from work to prepare for the festivities.

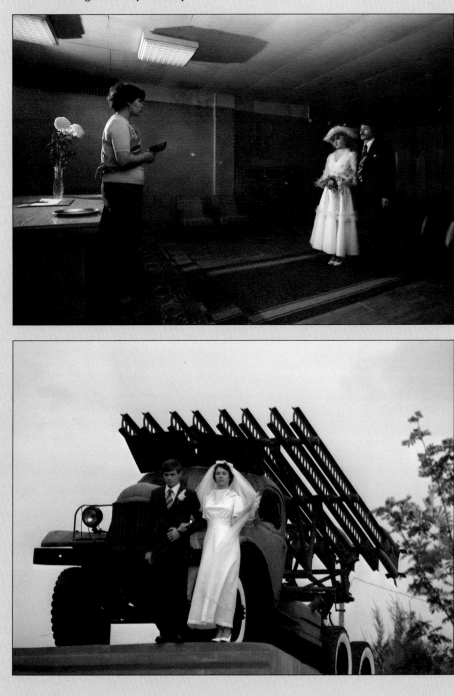

Following a recent custom, a bridal doll is attached to the car used by the wedding party. Brides prefer traditional white gowns; grooms usually wear dark business suits.

Newlyweds pose for obligatory photographs with the town's patriotic monument — here, a World War II rocket launcher. In Moscow, many couples leave flowers at Lenin's tomb.

as early as the age of three, when a child may enter preschool. Nearly half of all Soviet youngsters do. Some might already have spent two years in one of the state-run day-care centers set up to free mothers for jobs.

"The greatest offense a child can commit in kindergarten is to be different," observed an American journalist. From now on there is a right way and a wrong way to do everything, from eating to drawing a picture. "See how Mashenka holds her spoon," says a teacher to a child whose way with silverware is not acceptable. Or again, to a child who has drawn a large green flower with a little house under it: "Why don't you color the flower red or yellow? You've seen red or yellow flowers. And the building must be taller than the flower. Did you ever see a flower bigger than a building?"

Each year the strictures intensify to press conformity on the group. At the age of seven a Soviet child starts elementary school, the girls dressed in black or brown frocks, the boys in blue jackets with shoulder tabs. For the next three years, from 8:30 to 2:30, six days a week, they learn basic courses by rote, with a heavy emphasis on mathematics and science. Written work must be executed in ink, and handwriting must conform to the accepted penmanship style and be done with the right hand; left-handedness is discouraged.

In school the children become members of "links" in a juvenile collective. Each member's standing depends on the standing of the link, so that all watch over the performance and behavior of their fellows.

Dr. Urie Bronfenbrenner, a Cornell University sociologist who has studied Soviet education, described how the link system works with the example of

Concerned that city children may grow up without knowing the sounds of the outdoors, biophysicist Boris Veprintsev (*left*) goes to the birch forest near Moscow to capture the sounds on tape. His recordings have sold more than a million copies.

Vova, a boy brought before his link because he is doing badly in mathematics. "What did you do yesterday when you got home from school?" the link members ask him. In reply Vova dodges their attempts to probe his efforts on mathematics.

"A month ago you were warned to work harder on your math, and now you don't even mention it," says the chairman.

"I didn't have any math homework last night," explains Vova.

"You should have studied anyway," they tell him.

When a classmate suggests that two link members supervise Vova's home studies, he protests. "I don't need them. I can do it by myself."

"We have seen what you do by yourself," says the chairman. "Now we will work with you until you are ready to work alone."

Members of the link know the standing of each student because performance is graded constantly, on a scale of 1 to 5, in the student's daybook. "The daybook went up to the front of the

room when a student answered a question, and the teacher marked down a grade," explained the daughter of a Western journalist, who attended school in Moscow. "If a student got in trouble the teacher could ask for his daybook and write in a 2. At the bottom of each two facing pages, which represented a week, was a space for a weekly behavior grade and a grade for the neatness of the assignments listed in the book."

Once a week the daybook goes home for a parent's signature. If it contains criticism of the child's behavior, parents are expected to take responsibility for correcting it. Failure to do so can bring a summons from the teacher, or worse yet, the school may inform the parents' employers so that pressure now comes from the boss.

In the eighth year an examination determines which children will continue general studies and go on to a university, and which ones will enter a technical or vocational school. Only one out of five students is actually accepted at a university.

Candidates are winnowed out by competitive examinations that are supposed to give all segments of Soviet society equal opportunities for advancement but in fact often fail to achieve this egalitarian ideal. Theoretically, for example, 50 per cent of the students entering the prestigious Moscow University are supposed to be the children of peasants and factory workers, but in reality the figure is closer to 15 per cent. The rest are the children of writers, musicians, teachers, actors and party functionaries — privileged youngsters who gain special advantage because they generally attend special secondary schools. In addition, most of the university's students are ethnic Russians.

Most Soviet children are treasured, even overprotected: This rosy-cheeked youngster is almost lost from sight inside blankets and furs.

"One runs into an occasional Moldavian or Kazakh," says an observer, "but that is relatively rare."

Because a passing grade in the competitive examinations is a ticket to a better life, parents resort to various means, legal and illegal, to help their children. Those who can afford it—and some who cannot—hire private tutors to provide the winning edge. The cashier in a Moscow cafeteria complained to an acquaintance that she and her husband were giving up their annual vacation. "We have to be able to hire a coach for our oldest son so he'll have every chance to get into an institute," she said. Others use influence wherever it can be brought to bear, even passing a wad of rubles under the table to someone on the board of examiners. A few years ago the going rate for buying a pass-ing grade was reportedly 10,000 rubles.

When he reaches 18, every Soviet male owes his country two years of active military service—although for a university student this generally means taking officer reserve training to qualify as a junior lieutenant upon graduation. He then owes six months of service, which he can complete over the course of several summers. To repay the state for a university education, all graduates—male and female—are assigned jobs in their fields, often in remote Siberia, where the state is pushing development. Some, attracted by the pay and privileges granted for work on the frontier, settle there; but after the mandatory two-year stint, many look for jobs back in Moscow or Kiev or Leningrad, and pursue the good life.

Somewhere along this route, most young people pause to get married. In more than half of all Soviet weddings, both bride and groom are under 20. The ceremony is usually performed in a state-run Wedding Palace, and has been quick and proletarian, although recent efforts have attempted to glorify it with extra ritual.

Traditionally, Moscow newlyweds visit Red Square to lay a wreath on the Tomb of the Unknown Soldier or Lenin's tomb, and then hire a taxi or use a private car for a ride up to the Lenin Hills to have their picture taken against a panorama of central Moscow. The taxi is bedecked with ribbons, and on its grille hangs a small token of their wish for children: a bridal doll for a girl, a Teddy bear for a boy. "The children," well-wishers are likely to say, "they are our future."

A LOVE OF THE OUTDOORS

Perhaps it is the very discomfort of the climate — mostly cold and windy for months on end — that makes the Soviet people delight in living outdoors. The national game, chess, is played out in the parks in all but the worst weather; boisterous family celebrations are likely to be in a rustic front yard. Although many people live in towering apartments, on state farms as well as in cities, many others occupy individual, separate homes, each with a picket-fenced garden to bring within the family orbit the land loved so intensely.

Even the everyday chore of shopping, largely confined to the interiors of state shops, is more pleasant when it can be done out on the street, at stalls where farmers offer the freshest produce and meats, or at the corners where black marketeers sell scarce goods. But it is on holidays that the people of the Soviet Union can fully give in to their passion for the outdoors, carpeting beaches with their bodies, strolling through parks and sightseeing in the snow while the baby snuggles in a sled *(page 42)*.

Chess players pass a warm afternoon surrounded by onlookers in Moscow's Gorky Park. Chess has been played in the Soviet Union at least since the 10th Century.

At a dacha weekend retreat near Moscow, three generations celebrate a birthday with food, wine and guitar-accompanied song.

A mother leads her child past a single-family house, common in the countryside and villages. Most Russian couples today have only one offspring.

A block of new Moscow apartments, identical to those going up in many other cities, gleams behind a tenant's protectively wrapped car. The banner calls for worldwide Communist unity.

Despite a massive program of housing construction (two million dwelling units built per year), a fifth of the urban population must, like these women, double up. They and another woman share use of the kitchen.

THE CHALLENGE OF SHOPPING

On her work break, a woman buys meat from an outdoor stand. Such stands are set up around Moscow by the state stores to alleviate crowding in the shops themselves. Vendors usually wear armbands to indicate the store they represent.

Shopping bags in hand, Muscovites line up outside a store, waiting their turn to buy high-quality shoes. Such queues form mainly for exceptional goods but they may extend a block or more; one that existed for two days was made up of 10,000 to 15,000 people eager to buy carpets.

Patient shoppers wait in a state store to purchase fruit

38

from clerks who calculate prices on abacuses. Food is available in ample quantities; one result is a generation two to three inches taller than the parents.

Some of the 3.5 million vacationers who come annually to Sochi on the Black Sea, many as guests of their unions, crowd a black pebble beach.

Stylishly dressed young women dance together at a resort hotel while a potential male partner sits to one side.

A study in concentration, warmly clad Moscow fishermen seated on the frozen river wait for tugs on their lines. They have used the augers at right to drill holes through the thick ice.

A group of Soviet tourists who brought along a baby in a wicker sled pause to admire the sights on a winter outing near Moscow. In the distance is the 13th Century monastery of Suzdal, now preserved as a national monument.

Strolling in one of the "park rings" encircling Moscow, a young family projects the new Soviet chic. On the bench sits a more traditionally dressed "babushka," or "grandmother."

A wan winter sun lights a snowy
stretch of the Soviet Union's Baltic
coast. From October to March,
Moscow receives an average of only 15
minutes of sunshine a day.

AN IMMENSE AND RICH LAND

The most astounding feature of the Soviet Union is its size. Almost all of the United States, Canada and Mexico could fit within its borders. The U.S.S.R. is the largest political entity on earth, stretching 6,800 miles across two continents and through 11 time zones. Altogether, it spans a third of the Northern Hemisphere. To cross it by train takes seven days on the famed Trans-Siberian Railway (travelers making the trip come prepared with supplies of beer and vodka, meat pies and cold fish, cheese and fruit). Leningrad is closer to Montreal in Canada than it is to Vladivostock, the Trans-Siberian's final stop in the East.

Lenin himself had the opportunity to clock some of this stupendous distance when he was sent into Siberian exile by a tsarist court. "Neither towns nor dwellings," he noted gloomily as his train rattled eastward, "only a very few villages, and an occasional wood, but the rest all steppe . . . for three whole days."

A popular patriotic song likens the Soviet citizen to a landlord proudly striding across his domain. And indeed he has reason for pride. That land contains an unequaled plenitude of the substances people covet: an estimated one fourth of the earth's energy reserves, a prospector's bonanza of minerals, seemingly endless forests, and great tracts of fertile soil.

In location on the globe, however, the U.S.S.R. is not nearly so fortunate.

One third of it lies north of the temperate zone. (The offshore islands of Severnaya Zemlya are only 800 miles from the North Pole.) The interior is so far from the oceans that any ameliorating effect they might have on the climate is soon lost. As a result, the Soviet Union endures some of the worst winter weather in the world.

A close look at this immense land, from Old Russia in the West to the Pacific coast in the East, reveals how nature has helped to shape the Soviet Union of today.

About a quarter of the country is in Europe; the rest sprawls across Asia, with the low-lying Ural Mountains forming the dividing line between the two parts. The Asian section alone is larger than the United States — Alaska and Hawaii included. The European portion, running 1,800 miles from the Barents Sea in the North to the Caspian Sea in the South, consists of a gigantic plain, through which four major rivers flow — the Volga, Don, Dnieper and Dniester. The longest of these, the Volga, empties into the Caspian, the largest inland sea in the world.

If there is a single word to characterize the geography of the Soviet Union, *flat* is it. Three quarters of the land is less than 1,800 feet above sea level. The country's only tall mountains are in the Caucasus range — which contains Europe's highest peak, 18,480-foot Mount Elbrus — and in the Pamir mountains of southern Central Asia, where Com-

2

In a land with much snow but few hills for sledding, slides like this one were once immensely popular. They were constructed of wood and stood 30 to 40 feet tall.

munism Peak rears to 24,547 feet.

The monotony of landscape is offset north to south by the variety of vegetation zones. Winding in a broad band across the Arctic is the tundra, a semidesert where only mosses, lichens and stunted shrubs grow. It occupies 15 per cent of the country's entire land mass. At its southern limits, still above the Arctic Circle, the tundra gradually gives way to a zone where trees grow in ever-increasing numbers until they form the taiga, the dark and silent realm of spruce, larch and pine.

The taiga is the largest of the several zones and covers most of Siberia, as well as a large chunk of European Russia. Where the climate warms slightly, conifers cease to dominate and mixed forest takes over; this, in turn, surrenders to deciduous trees that thin out in their southern reaches, yielding to steppe grassland. Steppe encompasses most of the southern half of European Russia and rolls eastward deep into Siberia. At its southern edge, where precipitation is too low to support grass, patches of semidesert appear. And in Soviet Central Asia — the large bulge of land abutting Iran, Afghanistan and China — there are true deserts, as dry and bleak as any on earth.

Buried in this ground lies a prodigious wealth of minerals. The Soviet Union possesses one third of all the world's proven coal reserves and confidently expects to find, by the time its geologists are finished probing, that it has two thirds. That would be enough to supply the country with energy for more than 7,000 years at current rates of consumption. In the meantime, the U.S.S.R. has already become one of the world's top coal producers.

Geologists reckon Soviet oil reserves to be the world's largest. The Russians

have been aware for nearly a century that they possessed a lot of oil; fields in the Caucasus region were pumping half the global oil supply before World War I, and they are still producing. More recently the Soviets have begun to tap the even richer fields of Siberia. One region there is believed to contain 14 billion barrels, as much as lies beneath the North Sea.

During Stalin's time the oil was left pretty much undisturbed and coal was burned instead. Since then, the U.S.S.R. has become the world's greatest producer, pumping almost 12 million barrels a day — more than twice Saudi Arabia's output in 1983 — and accounting for almost 20 per cent of the entire world supply. Of this, three million barrels a day are exported.

In keeping with the abundance of oil, the Soviet Union's reserves of natural gas are thought to be about 40 per cent of the earth's total, more than three and a half times those of the United States. One field near the Arctic Circle may represent the world's highest concentration in a single area. To exploit its gas and oil, the U.S.S.R. has been building pipelines at a feverish pace, including a gigantic one running across most of Siberia and all of European Russia and into Western Europe.

The forests that cover so much of the Soviet land are another major energy source, providing heat for many rural homes. Not surprisingly, the country is the world's foremost producer of wood products. It fells and dresses about 13 billion cubic feet of timber every year, equal to the entire production of Canada and Europe. Marshy parts of forested areas offer another harvestable resource — peat. The U.S.S.R. contains 60 per cent of the world's peat reserves. Made up of decomposed vegetable matter, the peat is cut in blocks, dried and burned as a low-grade fuel, mostly to generate electricity.

As if coal, oil, gas, wood and peat were not enough to satisfy energy needs for years to come, the U.S.S.R. also has been developing its nuclear energy potential; more than a dozen nuclear energy plants were in operation by the early 1980s. Nor is water power neglected. The country contains an estimated 12 per cent of the world's hydroelectric sources. A single dam across the mile-wide Volga at Volgograd spins 22 turbines that put out 11.5 billion kilowatt hours of electricity every year; it is one of the biggest hydroelectric plants in all Europe.

This abundance of present and future energy can be put to work on half the world's store of iron ore, among other raw materials. The deposits of manganese, which is needed for alloys, are unmatched anywhere. And there is no lack of other minerals essential to modern technology: chromite, tungsten, titanium, molybdenum, nickel, cobalt, copper, lead, zinc, asbestos, mercury, antimony, silver, platinum, gold and diamonds. Indeed, the deposits of diamonds and gold in the Soviet Union are thought to be greater than those in South Africa. The blue kimberlite diamond pipes in the far Siberian North yield 12 million carats a year.

Resources for agriculture are as important as those for industry. Here the wealth in some essentials is outweighed by deficiencies in others. Of fertile soil and moisture, there is plenty, though not always where needed most. Of sunshine and warmth, however, there is generally too little.

The U.S.S.R. possesses around 550 million acres of arable land, and most of it is seeded to one crop or another every year. By contrast, the United States has a hundred million fewer acres of cultivable land, and seeds only three fourths of that total. Yet the U.S.S.R. cannot grow enough food to feed its own people, whereas the United States is able to supply not only itself but often other nations as well, including the U.S.S.R. Historically the Soviet Union has averaged one poor harvest out of every three; between 1979 and 1984 there were six disappointing harvests in a row.

Most Soviet agriculture is concentrated west of the Urals in Europe. This is the core of the nation, home to most of its people and locus of the government. Here lie three of the greatest cities — Moscow, Leningrad and Kiev, centers of transport and industry. South and west of Moscow, trending northward from the shores of the Black Sea and the Sea of Azov, in the Ukraine, the Crimea and Belorussia, spreads the soil so renowned for its fertility that its name in Russian, *chernozem*, meaning

A WORLD LEADER IN MINERALS

The wealth of the Soviet Union's natural resources is indicated by this comparison of Soviet output of minerals and fossil fuels with that of its closest competitors.

Although South Africa may produce more gold, and Zaire more diamonds — gem and industrial quality — the U.S.S.R. leads the world in production of coal, oil and iron ore. It is also the world's largest oil exporter — shipping more than three million barrels a day to Eastern Europe, Cuba and Western Europe.

MID-1980s

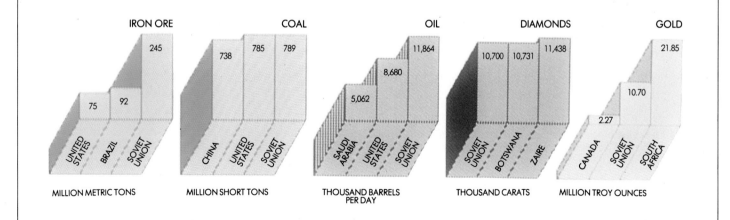

West of Moscow, in Belorussia,
a harvesting machine digs peat —
decomposed vegetable matter
used for fuel — from marshy land.
Nearly half the Soviet Union's peat
is found in this region.

"black earth," is applied to similar soils in other countries.

Such fertility often fails because the growing season is frustratingly brief. It lasts only four to six months, compared with eight to nine months for Western Europe. The Gulf Stream, which does so much to warm Western Europe, brings little benefit to the Soviet heartland. What damp, warm air approaches from the northwest quickly cools as it moves across the plains. And the rains it brings fall all too often at the wrong time. Drought — or the opposite, too much moisture — plays havoc with the fields. Sometimes torrential storms strike when the grain is ripe and heavy, leaving the precious crop a soggy ruin.

Moisture for crops is a problem over much of the Soviet Union, even though the country gets about 13 per cent of the world's runoff of fresh water, the most generous allotment of any nation on earth. The trouble is that 65 per cent of the supply flows northward, away from the agricultural regions and the warm but arid areas that might be made productive through irrigation. Two of the largest rivers in the European U.S.S.R., the Pechora and the Onega, and three of Siberia's, the Ob, the Yenisei and the Lena, spill their contents into the Arctic Ocean.

The Volga is the largest of the rivers that follow a southerly course, and it is the one most drastically redirected through a series of dams, primarily to furnish hydroelectric power for industry but also to irrigate farmland. A succession of 12 reservoirs impounds water with a total surface area of approximately 11,000 square miles.

By the 1970s, the Soviets had succeeded in irrigating more than three million acres in the northern Caucasus and other sizable areas in the South

with water from the Volga. In the planning stage are irrigation projects that will double the total acreage under cultivation in this region. Rice is the principal crop in the newly watered land, which yields more than half the country's consumption of that grain.

This extensive tinkering with nature has had a price. The systems of locks and dams on the Volga and other rivers have slowed river traffic on these major transport routes and made the rafting of cut timber more difficult and expensive. Much worse in ultimate effect is the heavy loss of water through evaporation from the huge reservoirs that lie behind the dams. Along with the quantity drained off for agricultural and industrial uses, evaporation has sharply reduced the end flow into the great lakes to the south — the Aral and Caspian Seas. Both of them have been shrinking; the Caspian alone dropped 30 feet in 50 years.

In addition, waste discharged by

upriver industries around Baku on the Caspian's southwestern coast have polluted the downstream areas and taken a toll on fishing, once a major industry there. Especially hard hit has been the sturgeon, the great Caspian fish that can grow up to 13 feet long, weigh more than a ton and live two or three hundred years. It provides the most renowned of Soviet delicacies, caviar.

The sturgeon swim up the Volga to lay their prized eggs. But as the river became increasingly polluted and more dams were built, fewer and fewer fish could complete the journey. The catch has decreased by half since the end of World War II.

Pollution controls subsequently cleaned up the water, and elevators made of wire were installed to lift the fish over the dams and upriver to the spawning grounds. (The elevator at the Volgograd dam is designed to carry some 60,000 sturgeon in a season; it once stalled when 40 tons of the fish

Framed by rocky outcrops, one
of Armenia's ancient churches stands
isolated on land now given over to
cultivation. On the horizon can be seen
the buildings of a state farm.

crowded aboard at once.) Although these measures have halted the decline in spawning sturgeon, the production of caviar remains less than either the Soviet fishermen or the world's epicures would like.

Such drawbacks to irrigation schemes did not prevent the Soviets from considering plans for a far more ambitious project — nothing less than the reversal of the direction of flow of northbound rivers. For at least 50 years scientists have speculated about that monumental turnaround. The most recent idea, now apparently shelved, would have required 30 to 50 years to complete, and would have remade the land on both sides of the Urals. In European Russia three north-flowing rivers, the Onega, the Northern Dvina and the Pechora, were to have been shifted into reverse, their flow diverted into the southbound Volga by means of dikes, dams and pumping stations.

On the eastern side of the Urals, the Ob River — the fourth largest in the world, known to Siberians as the grandmother of rivers — was to have been dammed just below its confluence with a branch called the Irtysh. Water from the enormous reservoir thus created would then have been channeled southward to refresh the dying Aral Sea and to irrigate parched lands of Kazakhstan and Uzbekistan. At one stage, engineers contemplated carrying the water through a canal 900 miles long, to be dug in part by nuclear blasting, but protests from within and outside the Soviet Union forced abandonment of that idea. Instead the water was to move through ancient river beds that were discovered on satellite photographs and that coincide with a natural depression called the Turgay Trough.

If these grandiose proposals were ever carried out, they would constitute the most colossal engineering works undertaken by any people anywhere. They would displace thousands of Soviets, drown ancient towns and hamlets, and impose ecological costs still beyond measuring, perhaps even altering the climate of the Northern Hemisphere.

The shelving of the scheme has produced disappointment for some. The Soviets have seen the effects of irrigation on 16 million acres in the southern regions of Kazakhstan and Turkmenistan in Soviet Central Asia. Herculean

effort and an intricate system of dams, reservoirs and canals have made the sands bloom. In scattered artificial oases grow cotton, rice, tobacco, sugar beets, wheat and fruit. An industrial infrastructure including textile factories has sprung up to process what the soil produces. If the northbound rivers were turned around to run the other way, another 150 million acres could be seeded in this region.

To the obstacles nature has set in the way of farming must be added those arising from human action. The social and economic system of agriculture established by the Soviet regime has a profound effect on farm output, and some Western analysts hold the system largely to blame for the country's failure to meet food requirements.

Stalin's first Five-Year Plan, inaugurated in 1928, called for total collectivization of agriculture under direct state control. The government seized ownership and operation of all farms, overriding violent resistance from many peasants, especially from the most productive and prosperous of them, the *kulaks*. Millions of *kulaks* were either

killed or arrested and sent to Siberia.

The state undertook to manage all aspects of agriculture from Moscow. Quotas for the production of various crops were set by headquarters; managers (some sent out for the job) were installed; harvests were collected and sent to state-owned processing plants or to state markets for sale to consumers. Total state control proved too rigid, however, and after a few years it was loosened somewhat; all farm workers were also allowed to cultivate private plots, producing whatever they wished to sell in free, competitive markets at prices higer than those set by the state. This secondary system — largely government-run but allowing for some individual enterprise — has continued with only minor modifications since the 1930s.

Official figures document the lackluster record of Soviet farming. In 1984 about 20 million people — 20 per cent of the working population — were engaged in agriculture. Comparisons with other countries are difficult because of differences in how statistics are compiled. In the United States, 3 per

cent of the labor force works at farming, but this figure includes only those actually tilling the soil and excludes support workers — specialists such as mechanics who repair machinery. Some of the extra workers are counted as agricultural workers in the U.S.S.R.

Yet despite the incompatibility of statistics, certain measures do seem revealing. Soviet agriculture is heavily mechanized but appears to be more labor-intensive than is usual in Western countries. As nearly as can be worked out, 55 hours of labor are needed to bring 220 pounds of beef to market in the U.S.S.R., 39 hours for pork. In the U.S. the equivalent numbers would be 3.1 hours and 1.3 hours. Of course, climate, as well as the Soviet system, must bear some of the blame for these and other shortfalls. Because winter lasts so long, livestock is kept indoors for at least two months more than in Western Europe. Feed that might otherwise be used to fatten grazing animals for the slaughter is thus spent maintaining them through the coldest months.

Where the influence of the system shows up most clearly, perhaps, is in

A 10,000-acre state farm, one of 21,000 in the Soviet Union, spreads across the Belorussian landscape. Salaried workers — who live in the prefabricated apartment buildings below — tend 11,000 head of cattle.

comparisons of the productivity of state-controlled agriculture versus that of the farmers' private plots. The individual plots are gardens of no more than one and one third acres each. They account for just 3 per cent of the total area sown to crops. Yet they yield 66 per cent of the potatoes grown in the Soviet Union and 33 per cent of the vegetables, meat and eggs.

Official agriculture, by contrast, is large in scale. There are two types of these farms: Collectives, called *kolkhozes*, and state farms, called *sovkhozes*.

The *kolkhozes* are like cooperatives; workers are paid in kind with a share of the crop and animal output. They are also paid a cash sum that is distributed after all expenses incurred by the collective are paid. The money is divided up according to the amount and type of work done, measured in "labor-day units." The state farms are "factories in the field," employing workers who draw straight salaries based on rates established by the government. The state farms also seem to be larger than the collectives (covering an average of 50,000 acres, whereas the *kolkhozes*

average only 15,000 acres), but this difference is deceptive: The areas seeded to crops and the numbers of farm workers tilling the fields tend to be about the same on both types of farm.

The main emphasis in Soviet agriculture is specialization. Although the collectives raise a variety of produce and livestock, state farms tend to be more mechanized and to concentrate on a single commodity, such as grain or fruit. Specialization extends to the labor force on both types of farm: Work groups are organized into brigades and are responsible for only one phase of the farm's operation, such as crop seeding or harvesting. Smaller teams, the *zven'ia*, are the lowest level of a work force on a farm and are, in many cases, headed by women. These teams usually concentrate on such specific chores as feeding pigs or milking cows.

The collectives are made up of family units, and membership in the *kolkhoz* is a birthright. One *kolkhoz* may include as many as several thousand families, but the average is 440. Generally the families live in villages near their fields, occupying cottages called *izby*. The *izby*

lack indoor plumbing and central heating but have electricity. They possess a certain cluttered coziness — lace curtains at the windows, windowsills overflowing with house plants, and possibly a draped icon in one corner. However, the *izby* are gradually being replaced by concrete apartment buildings or individual houses equipped with modern amenities; some peasant villages now look much like Western suburbs.

On the state farms, particularly in the prosperous areas of Europe, workers generally live in apartments similar to those provided for their counterparts in industry. They also get many of the services — good schools, day nurseries, cultural activities — that other factories supply employees. These perquisites make life on the state farms attractive to families. However, many young people, frustrated by isolation and lacking any rights to the land, take advantage of opportunities to get jobs elsewhere, and they leave.

While the great state farms and the big collectives of the black-earth country in Europe amount to a mechanized, mass-production food industry, the

system of socialized agriculture in less
favored areas sometimes disintegrates,
and both life and production can become grim indeed. In the late 1960s, a
dissident Moscow writer, Andrei Amalrik, documented such a situation after
he was banished to a struggling *kolkhoz*
in western Siberia.

The farm had been carved from the
taiga, and in spring the *kolkhozniki*
planted wheat, oats, corn, potatoes, clo-
ver and flax in the soggy earth. Flax
and dairy products from 150 cows were
supposed to be the money crops. But in
Amalrik's first season of exile the flax
harvest was a failure. Crews neglected
to dry the seed so it could be made into
linseed oil, and because there were in-
sufficient people to card the flax stems
for the linen mill, most of the crop was
left to rot in the fields. The cows were
supposed to be milked by machine, but
frequently the machines broke down.
Pipes intended to bring water to the
barns were rusted out, and nobody
bothered to replace them.

Most of the workers lived in tumble-
down *izby*. They swore a lot. They quar-
reled a lot. And they drank a lot —
home-brewed beer so potent that
"three mugs were enough to knock a
man out" or home-distilled vodka,
made of rye rather than potatoes and
"muddy green in color."

Today, the rugged life on Amalrik's
Siberian *kolkhoz* is perhaps less typical
of that disproportionately large and
mostly empty part of the Soviet Union
than was the case in earlier times. Siberia is still a place to send prisoners and
still a frontier, but it is booming. Not
only does the region have 60 per cent of
the nation's timber, but it also holds 60
per cent of the coal, the greatest share
of valuable minerals, quantities of rare
and costly furs, and huge herds of rein-

**Proud of her snug cottage, a
Ukrainian farm woman leans against a
pillow-decked bed that doubles as a
sofa. She has spread fresh grass on the
floor and suspended boughs from
the ceiling in observance of Pentecost.**

53

deer that yield meat, milk and leather.

One of the major problems implicit in Siberia's size is distance. The inescapable demands of moving people and things from one faraway place to another are extraordinarily difficult to meet in the ill-favored terrain and savage weather. About a third of Siberia is almost entirely without road or railroad. The only long-haul paved highway in Siberia takes off from the town of Never, a stop on the Trans-Siberian Railroad 500 miles east of Lake Baikal, and heads straight north through the Stanovoy Mountains to Aldan, a gold-mining town, and on up to Yakutsk, a distance of roughly 700 miles.

With the uncovering of more and more of Siberia's riches, however, rails are being pushed into Asia. Where once the only steel track across the empty hinterland was the meandering Trans-Siberian, there is now a growing network that reaches from Vladivostok nearly to Lake Baikal just above the Mongolian border, south to the city of Alma-Ata in the shadow of the snow-covered Tien Shan range, and north to the outpost of Vorkuta above the Arctic Circle in the Pechora Basin.

Improved transport is one indication of the rapid development of Siberia, particularly around the unique Lake Baikal. The scimitar-shaped lake, 400 miles long and roughly 50 wide, is the world's most capacious fresh-water basin. It is also the deepest — a little more than a mile deep at one point. Formed 25 million years ago, it is home to 600 species of plants and twice as many kinds of animals, including some found nowhere else on earth. Among them are the world's only fresh-water seals.

Two cities stand on Baikal's shores. The smaller, Ulan Ude on the southeastern littoral, is the capital of the Buryat region. The other, Irkutsk, straddles Baikal's only outlet into the north-flowing Angara, which eventually joins the Yenisei and spills into the Kara Sea and Arctic Ocean. Before the coming of industry, neither settlement had an adverse effect on the lake, but now sewage and pollutants are jeopardizing the water's purity.

Irkutsk was founded in 1652 by rebellious Cossacks who came here partly to get out from under the Tsar's thumb — but even more to place the native huntsmen under theirs. The Cossacks were the original exploiters of Siberia's wealth, then believed to consist only of the splendid pelts of wild animals. Irkutsk became a major fur trading center, and today it is probably the fur capital of the world. Its great warehouses are hung with pelts of white and silver fox, squirrel, ermine, mink, sable, polar bear, wildcat, otter and muskrat. In the old days, these animals were all taken by individual hunters; some still are, by private trappers licensed by the government. But now most kinds of fur animals, particularly silver fox and mink, are raised in cages. Like agriculture, the fur industry has come to be a collective enterprise.

The most highly prized furs are said to come from the Barguzin hills above Lake Baikal. The black Barguzin sable is still honored as the king of fur animals, and is still largely hunted in the wild: The animals do not reproduce easily in captivity. Even today some of the hunters follow their traplines through the snowy taiga on sleds drawn by reindeer, but others are ferried by helicopter. Purists go after the sable with dogs trained to employ a "tender" mouth to avoid damaging the skin. "When you follow a sable," said one hunter, "he can go anywhere — into trees, among rocks. The hunter dresses lightly because he must run all the time. He takes care to stay with his dogs, so that the sable will not burrow into the snow" before he can shoot it.

In the 1980s the official income of the Soviet fur trade was more than $100 million a year. How much poachers earned from black-market sales cannot be estimated, but their profits were surely less than in the good old days of the fur trade in the 17th Century, when a prime black fox pelt could bring its captor a cabin, 55 acres of land, five horses, 40 head of cattle and a few dozen barnyard fowl.

When Irkutsk's principal industry was the fur trade, the city's inhabitants lived in log houses, their window and door frames and gables enhanced by elaborately cut moldings. In the 1960s many of the picturesque houses succumbed to the bulldozer as concrete-slab apartments were built for 50,000 workers imported to convert the pristine Baikal into a gigantic power source. Two of the world's mightiest dams, the first at the Irkutsk outlet of the Angara River and the second downstream at Bratsk, were equipped with turbines to provide electricity for huge aluminum and wood-processing plants set on Baikal's shores.

It took 13 years to build the dams and the industrial complexes. But even before they were finished, they raised a storm of public outrage unheard of in the Soviet Union. Angry citizens, foreseeing pollution of the lake and destruction of the taiga, protested. "We are destroying our home," said Leonid Leonov, one of the Soviet Union's revered writers. "Baikal is not only a priceless basin of living water but also a part of our souls." One concern was the lake's unique crustaceans, the tiny

Home from a successful hunt, a Siberian of the forested Altai region shakes out sable pelts while a companion examines fox skins. True sable exists only in the Soviet Union; about 100,000 pelts are sold each year.

epishura, which, by filtering 250,000 tons of calcium from the lake waters each year, guarantee its unparalleled clarity. Even Moscow listened, and equipment was installed to purify the industries' wastes. Despite these efforts, many ecologists remain pessimistic; a report of the U.S.S.R. Academy of Sciences, wrote one expert, suggested that "the danger of Baikal being destroyed had increased rather than decreased," adding, "the entire lake was on the brink of irreversible changes."

Baikal lies at about lat. 57° N., and the lake by November wears a four-foot-thick covering of ice. At that point, the ice can be used for the transport of people and goods aboard trucks and sleds. Unhappily, the ice has a tendency to split into crevasses without warning. Many people in the area believe that the best way to travel Baikal's ice is by horse and sled, because if a crack suddenly opens, the animal will jump across it, pulling the sled over the break.

However cold the Baikal area may be in winter, it seems semitropical compared with the region farther north where gold, diamonds and oil lie; indeed, Irkutsk has come to be regarded as a favorite retirement city by workers living on the frigid northern frontier, where the temperature has been known to drop to below −90° F.

In this region, as in almost half of the Soviet Union, the surface is underlain by permanently frozen ground — permafrost. Occasionally, the permafrost exposes the remains of woolly mammoths, extinct relatives of the elephant, that were frozen whole in it during the last Ice Age; the stomach contents of one of these deep-frozen mammoths showed that the animal had been browsing on buttercups just before its death.

In some regions the permafrost extends a mile down. During the brief northern summers, it may thaw to a depth of six feet, turning the surface into a quagmire that can swallow trucks, tractors and other machines.

As an example of the destructive power of permafrost, Marina Gavrilova, a senior scientist at the Eternal Frost Institute in Yakutsk, told what happened to one of the first power

55

2

In a village near Irkurtsk in eastern Siberia, vendors sell milk frozen around wooden handles so that it can be carried home. Temperatures remain well below zero throughout Siberia during winter, but rise to as high as 100° F. in summer.

dams built in this frigid area. "The engineers," she said, "were sure their hundreds of thousands of tons of concrete would withstand any stress of nature. An earthquake would probably not have hurt their dam, but its weight melted the frozen rocks on which it stood. The rocks crumbled and the dam split open."

In Yakutsk, as elsewhere in Siberia, buildings must be raised on stilts to allow the cold air to circulate under them; otherwise, even the minimal heat seeping from their floors would thaw the top layer of permafrost and cause the structures to subside or tilt. Siberia is full of old structures that now lean every which way; one traveler reported seeing a house that had sunk up to its windowsills.

New construction techniques prevent such listing. In one method, the frozen ground is melted with a steam hose; then 30-foot reinforced-concrete piles are jackhammered into the muck, where they freeze fast forever.

Another trick is to use a pile containing pipes filled with kerosene (which will not freeze solid at the temperature of the frozen ground). To set the fluid-filled pile, the kerosene is heated so that the pile melts its own path down into the permafrost. Then the heat is turned off, allowing the ground to refreeze around the pile and clamp it tight. The kerosene is not pumped out but remains inside the pile.

Over the long winter, the kerosene is circulated by convection currents set up by temperature differences between ground level and the pile bottom, deep down. Because the ground is then colder near the surface than below, the kerosene at the bottom of the pile is warmer than the fluid near the top; it rises while the colder fluid falls, thus keep-

ing all the fluid well-chilled. In summer, this circulation stops, but the season of warm surface temperatures is so short, and the kerosene has been chilled to such a low temperature during the winter, that the fluid keeps the ground around the pile frozen at all times — and the pile is held firmly anchored summer and winter.

Winter is a cruel king. "In Siberia," goes a saying, "forty degrees below zero is not a frost, a hundred kilometers is not a distance, half a liter of vodka is not a drink and forty years is not a woman." Tires burst from the cold, steel shatters like ice and rivers freeze to a depth of 20 feet.

Yet some laborers manage to work outdoors in midwinter; mortar is heated so brick can be laid in the freezing air. "The cold," wrote a visitor to Yakutsk, "makes the newcomer aware of his nose for the first time; every hair inside freezes rigid in a second. You can actually feel them bending with each intake of breath. Naturally you can see your breath, but what is more extraordinary, you can hear it turn to ice." One effect of this phenomenon is "people mist," a sort of luminescent smog that is produced over Yakutsk by the moist emanations of human bodies and the exhaust of automobiles. Engines are kept running 24 hours a day to prevent them from freezing solid, and windshields are double-glazed against the frost.

Schools are not closed unless the temperature sinks below −60° F. In homes, people live behind thick walls with triple storm doors and windows three panes thick. Women wear three to six layers of wool tights, and men pile on garments; no one carries metal coins in pants pockets. Leather would freeze and crack within minutes, so everybody

56

Offering a view of a wintry landscape, this window in a Siberian home is shielded by a sheet of glass with a strip of cotton batting stuffed between to block drafts. Unlike most, the window does not open; generally one of the small panes is hinged for ventilation.

wears felt or reindeer-fur boots and totes shoes for indoor wear in a parcel.

Drinking water is delivered to the home in solid chunks sawed out of the river, or is channeled through above-ground pipes that must be heated every few yards to keep their contents flowing. Milk is sold in brick form, with wood handles inserted so that it can be carried home easily. Food is stored in bags hung outside windows, where it freezes and can be used as needed. A favorite delicacy is raw, frozen fish, served in thin crystalline pieces with suet, mustard or other accompaniments. A visitor who tried it found the slices without much taste, "but it was amusing to crunch them like candies."

This is the land of the "long ruble," where workers are paid extra for services performed in brutal weather. The long ruble varies with climate and distance but follows a typical scale: 40 per cent above the going rate elsewhere just for taking the job, another 10 per cent after six months, double salary or even more for those who stick it out five years, annual vacations of 42 days and, every other year, a round-trip ticket to anywhere in the U.S.S.R.

Long-ruble country is also young people's country; the average age of Siberiaks — transplants from Mother Russia — is 29. The rugged environment and distance from civilization do not prevent an active social and cultural life. There are movies, theater, ballet practically as elegant as in Moscow, symphony orchestras, nightclubs and television beamed in from Moscow by satellite. The cost of making Siberia livable as well as productive is high, but the potential return is higher yet. In the biggest land on earth, the biggest region — recalcitrant though it may be — holds inestimable promise.

RAILROAD OF YOUNG HEROES

"The construction project of the century" is what the U.S.S.R. calls its newest railroad, the $14 billion BAM—Baikal-Amur Mainline. The boast is justified. BAM stretches 2,000 miles from a point west of Siberia's Lake Baikal to the Amur River on the Pacific coast, crossing seven mountain ranges and spanning more than 3,700 gorges, swamps, streams and rivers. For two thirds of the way, the heavy-duty tracks were laid over permafrost, frozen ground that can thaw and heave. They also crossed one of the most earthquake-prone regions in the world; as many as 2,000 tremors a year buckle the tracks and cause landslides.

BAM is the latest "hero project"—a huge, demanding task undertaken to impress the world and inspire the Soviet people. Thousands of young workers laid about a quarter mile of track a day completing the link-up in October 1984. Work will continue in the tunnels until 1990. Where in the early '70s there was wilderness, a decade later there was not only railroad, but more than 60 boomtowns—and the dream of opening Siberia to development was closer to reality.

Bulldozers prepare a site for a prefabricated bridge; behind them runs the broad swath cut through virgin birch and pine forest for the Baikal-Amur Mainline.

A traveling advertisement for the new Baikal-Amur Mainline covers the side of one of the red-painted cars of the old Trans-Siberian Railroad, with which the BAM connects.

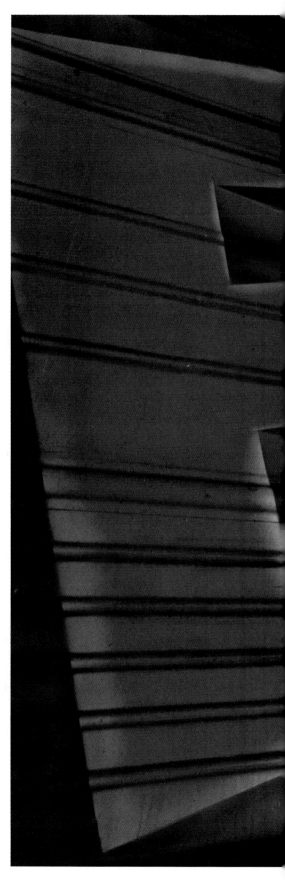

Siberian Yakuts — part of the labor force drawn from the local population — lay a prefabricated section of track with the aid of a crane.

Members of a work gang lever a section of track into place. Some BAM wages are three times the national norm. Women — here in kerchiefs — receive the same pay as the men.

Visiting musicians from Latvia put on a trackside concert for BAM workers during a rest break.

Working in glare-lit mud, laborers
complete the three-quarter-mile-long
Nagornyy tunnel after years of
drilling through granite and ice.

Gloveless mechanics use gasoline
that has been heated to thaw and wash
chilled parts of a drill.

At temperatures of − 50° F. or lower, truck engines must be left running day and night — or be warmed up by fires lighted under them.

Where insulating moss and lichens
have been destroyed by construction
work, the permafrost melts and
becomes a bog. Long-term effects of
such changes in the pristine
ecology of Siberia are unknown.

Newly laid tracks buckle with the
heaving caused by frost action. In some
areas, the BAM's roadbed was built
six feet deep over the permafrost and
allowed to settle for two years
before trains could pass over it.

These faces from the Soviet
Union present a small sample of its
ethnic diversity: a Russian schoolgirl,
a Georgian farm woman and a
bemedaled Uzbek worker from Central
Asia. Today distinctions are lessened
by intermarriage and the imposition of
a common language, Russian.

A COUNTRY OF COUNTRIES

Most people the world over refer to the Soviet Union as Russia. Even Soviet citizens — who resent foreigners' use of the term — often call it by that name themselves. Its real name, the Union of Soviet Socialist Republics, mouthful though it is, reflects more nearly the country's human composition. It is not one country so much as many — a conglomeration of 15 different so-called union republics, 20 autonomous republics, 8 autonomous regions and 10 autonomous areas.

In the U.S.S.R. as a whole, there are more than 100 different ethnic groups, ranging from Russians and Latvians to Uzbeks and Yakuts, speaking no fewer than 80 different languages, writing in five different alphabets, practicing Islam, Judaism, Buddhism and 152 sectarian versions of Christianity, and sometimes failing to get along with one another.

Some of the political subdivisions correspond to ethnic homelands, but others do not; among the natives of the Uzbek republic, for example, are Turkomen, Tadzikhs and many other peoples. In the Soviet Union, ethnic background — which is generally translated as "nationality" — is just as important as citizenship, and practically all official documents, including the interior passport that everyone is required to carry, specify both.

A Western visitor to Moscow got a hint of this ethnic preoccupation when he commented to his guide on the many Russian tourists in Red Square. She quickly corrected him. "Those are not Russians," she sneered, "those are Soviets." Her tone explained why the U.S.S.R., despite its composite nature, is generally referred to as Russia. The Russians may be only one of 100 ethnic groups, but they dominate, in every activity, throughout every part of the huge Soviet territory.

The Russians are descendants of Slavic tribes who settled northern central Europe in prehistoric times and over the centuries mixed with various conquerors: Scandinavian, Lithuanian, Polish and German peoples from the west, and from the south and east Tartars (also called Mongols), Khazars and others. The Russians remain predominantly Slavic, and intensely proud of that heritage. They are the most numerous of the Soviet peoples, 140 million strong, making up 52 per cent of the population of 271 million.

In addition, it is the Russians who inhabit the largest of the 15 republics. Known officially as the Russian Soviet Federated Socialist Republic, or R.S.F.S.R., it spreads all the way from the Baltic Sea to the shores of the Pacific Ocean, encompasses approximately three quarters of the Soviet Union's total land mass, and is the site of the country's largest industrial centers and cities, including the national capital, Moscow.

3

The Russians' influence beyond the R.S.F.S.R. is obvious. Russian is taught in all the schools of the country, and the Moscow accent is now the standard for radio and television. About three quarters of the members of the Politburo, the ruling body, are Russian, and most key party jobs go to Russians.

In the 14 republics beyond the R.S.F.S.R., where non-Russians make up the majority of the population, control over local government is in the hands of the Russian representatives of the Communist Party. The top post —that of first Party secretary—is likely to be filled by a native inhabitant, but this person is generally a figurehead; the real power is wielded by the second Party secretary, who is virtually always a Russian, and by the local chief of the secret police, also a Russian. More often than not, neither of these Moscow representatives speaks the native language.

The Russians came to such dominance by first conquering the Slavic groups neighboring the Moscow region, and then going on to extend their country's borders until by 1881 it covered much the same territory as the U.S.S.R. does today, more than 100 years later.

In the process, they became masters of the multitude of peoples, Asians as well as Europeans, who continue to give the U.S.S.R. a rich diversity—and an inner pressure—unlike that of any other nation in the world. Some of these peoples are quite different from the Russians; others are much like them in appearance, life style and habits (Chapter 1). But even those who seem to be most similar display flavorful distinctions in outlook.

Just south and west of the Russian homeland is that of their close relatives,

the Ukrainians and Belorussians, both of them Slavic groups that have long been part of the Russian Empire. The Belorussians, numbering approximately 10 million, have been almost totally assimilated into Russian culture, but the Ukrainians remain passionately proud of their own unique heritage and they resent any Russian condescension toward them.

Indeed, the Ukrainians consider themselves more cultivated than the Russians, and never cease reminding them that the Ukrainian city of Kiev was the country's capital when Moscow was "a wheel track in the forest." There are 42 million Ukrainians, and they make a big contribution to Soviet life.

Kiev, which the Russians call "the mother of cities," is today the third-largest city in the Soviet Union. Heavily damaged during World War II, it has been restored as a handsome capital of culture, with poplar-lined avenues, the-

salt, is still offered to guests as a symbol of hospitality.

When French novelist Honoré de Balzac visited the Ukraine, more than a century ago, he observed, "I counted 77 ways of making bread." And when a Ukrainian heard of the Frenchman's comment, he added, "No one has counted all our cakes."

The Ukrainians, Belorussians and Russians form the Slavic nucleus of the country, making up 72 per cent of its population. All around them — and to some extent living among them — are peoples who differ not only in ethnic origin but also in culture.

To the west and north of the Russian region are the homelands of three Baltic peoples — Estonians, Latvians and Lithuanians — who specialize in fishing and dairy farming. The Baltic peoples, who enjoy the Soviet Union's highest standard of living, also are in general the most European in outlook. They use the Latin alphabet instead of the Russian Cyrillic one, and traditionally they have been Protestant or Roman Catholic, rather than Russian Orthodox. (Latvia has the only cardinal within the Soviet Union.)

Lithuania, the largest of the Baltic republics, has a population of three and a half million and a long and fascinating history. While Russia was evolving in isolation, Lithuanian armies were marching southward, absorbing parts of today's Ukraine and Belorussia and some of Russia itself.

In the 14th Century, Lithuania extended all the way from the Baltic to the Black Sea. In the 16th Century, it grew larger still through union with Poland. Not until 1795, after a weak and almost anarchic Poland was divided up among its stronger neighbors, did Lithuania become a part of Russia. Although it is

aters, an opera house, a symphony hall and Kiev University, with 6,000 students who prefer to speak and write Ukrainian over Russian.

Much of the color of the old Ukraine survives in the countryside, where comfortable white-washed mud-brick or stone houses with thatched roofs are hung with the elaborate embroidery for which the region is famous. Here is the rich, black topsoil that has made the Ukraine the breadbasket of the nation,

and now that sugar beets are a major crop, the sugar bowl as well. Here also are centers of the coal-mining, steel and chemical industries.

The Ukrainians have long known how to make the most of their bounty. "My grandmother always said," boasts one housewife, "that a girl should be able to sift flour before she can walk and make bread before she can talk." A platter-sized loaf of bread called a *khlib i sil,* its center cradling a mound of

still largely an agrarian region, Lithuania also has factories that turn out electronic equipment, appliances and half of the metal-cutting lathes that are produced in the Soviet Union.

Latvia, the second-largest of the Baltic republics, with 2.5 million inhabitants, is more heavily industrialized, producing such things as plastics, bicycles, telephones and ships. The Latvians lived under German influence for 500 years before being taken over by the Russians during the 18th Century. Yet through all of this they managed to cling to their customs and their language. And they are as fervently possessive of these today as they have ever been. Each summer thousands of people decked out in folk costumes gather in Riga to confirm their Latvian roots and to sing the ancient songs of their motherland.

The Estonians, who manufacture agricultural machinery, scientific instruments and textiles, retain a Scandinavian look with their blond hair and blue eyes, but they are not so closely related to the Scandinavians as they are to the Finns, their neighbors to the north. They are believed to be descendants of hunters from the Ural Mountains, far to the east, who settled their present homeland about 2,500 years ago; their language, like Finnish, is among the few in Europe that are not of the Indo-European group. Finland is just 50 miles away, across the Gulf of Finland, and Estonians watch Finnish television beamed from Helsinki.

Estonia's noisiest expression of cultural distinction is its *Laulupidu,* a song festival that originated in 1869 and is held every five years in a park near Tallinn, the capital. Some 30,000 singers crowd onto the big stage of the bandshell and sing Estonian folk songs for audiences that may number 200,000. "The first number is dedicated to Lenin," said one of the participants, "and the last song to the friendship of the Soviet peoples, but what is in between belongs to us."

The Baltic peoples, despite ethnic and linguistic differences, make up a socially and geographically distinct group within the U.S.S.R. Far to the south is another group who share many characteristics: the Georgians, Armenians and Azerbaijanians. They are descended from Middle Easterners, with a touch of the Tartars who overran their mountainous homelands centuries ago. The most famous of their sons is Josef Stalin, a Georgian.

These southern groups produce fruit, tea, hydroelectric power and, in the Baku fields, oil. Their contribution to the bubbling pot of Soviet ethnicity is rich, spicy and often puzzling to the northerners.

All three peoples are noted for freewheeling business activities that violate the spirit — and often the letter — of the Soviet law. An Azerbaijanian taxi driver candidly explained that he had made a 500-ruble payoff to a housing commissar to get his tiny, old-fashioned house. A modern apartment in one of the new high-rise buildings outside the city would have required a bribe beyond his means, he explained. When asked why he did not simply apply and get on the official waiting list, the cabbie was amused. The wait, he said, would be 20 to 30 years.

Pravda regularly prints disapproving stories about such illicit dealings. A construction cooperative was accused of having bulldozed an unauthorized new road over the Caucasus into the R.S.F.S.R. just so farmers would be able to dodge the "vegetable patrols" set up on the main highway by the authorities to put a stop to illegal transactions in food. Large amounts of money were at stake; at least one farm-

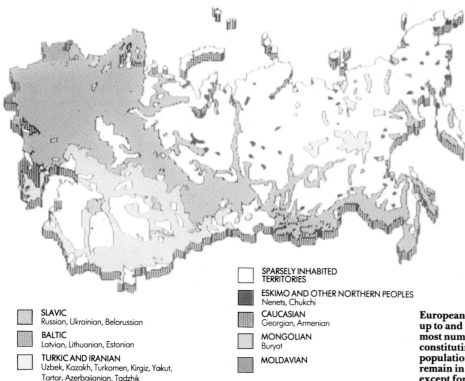

SPARSELY INHABITED
TERRITORIES

ESKIMO AND OTHER NORTHERN PEOPLES
Nenets, Chukchi

CAUCASIAN
Georgian, Armenian

MONGOLIAN
Buryat

MOLDAVIAN

SLAVIC
Russian, Ukrainian, Belorussian

BALTIC
Latvian, Lithuanian, Estonian

TURKIC AND IRANIAN
Uzbek, Kazakh, Turkmen, Kirgiz, Yakut, Tartar, Azerbaijanian, Tadzhik

European Slavs, who occupy areas up to and beyond the Urals, are the most numerous of Soviet peoples, constituting 72 per cent of the population. Most smaller groups remain in their ancient homelands — except for the Tartars, who live in many parts of the U.S.S.R.

er is known to have turned an illegal profit of 50,000 rubles, selling 10 tons of tangerines.

In 1973, a national scandal arose when a Georgian by the name of Otari Lazeishvili was accused of having pocketed a million rubles, money that should rightfully have gone to state organizations. The amount was actually much greater, say his countrymen, relishing the account of Lazeishvili's network of underground factories manufacturing such goods as turtleneck sweaters and trendy raincoats for his 100 collaborators to sell in black markets all across the Soviet Union.

Georgians are noted for their wine making — and for their hospitality. They take deep pleasure in food and drink. When a diner makes a wine selection in a Georgian restaurant, the waiter is likely to ask, "How many bottles?" This love of conviviality is traced, in one charming account, to the origin of the Georgian homeland. On the eighth day of Creation, goes this story, God parceled out the globe to the many peoples of the world. Once everyone was settled, God started for home, whereupon he encountered the Georgians. They were sitting around a table by the side of the road.

Shaking his head, God admonished them, "While you sat here eating and drinking, singing and joking, the whole world was divided up. Now nothing is left for you."

The leader of the Georgians, with true Georgian cunning, replied, "It was very wrong, we know. But God, while we enjoyed ourselves, we didn't forget you. We drank to you to thank you for making such a beautiful world."

"That's more than anybody else did," said God. "So I'll tell you what I'm going to do. I'm going to give you the last

Farm women harvest cabbage on a rocky Armenian hillside below an old stone church. The Armenian Apostolic Church, one of the most venerable of Christian denominations, has its own hierarchy and rituals, distinct from those of Russian Orthodoxy.

little corner of the world — the place I was saving for myself because it is most like Paradise."

The Georgians' neighbors to the south, the Armenians, have an equally colorful tale of the Creation. According to the Armenian account, by the time God got around to them while making his distribution of the earth's land, he had nothing left but rocks — and rocks are what they got. Theirs is a rugged, stark country with most of the arable land squeezed into the Aras Valley along the border with Turkey.

The Armenians, Azerbaijanians and Georgians claim to get a special bonus from living where they do — incredible longevity. The Soviet government calls the Caucasus a center of the *dolgozhiteli* (long-lifers), men and women who remain hale after more than 100 years. According to the Institute of Gerontology in Kiev, there are some 20,000 long-lifers in the U.S.S.R., a major portion of them in Georgia and Azerbaijan. Indeed, the government maintains that 39 out of every 100,000 Georgians and 44 of every 100,000 Azerbaijanians live past 100. *Pravda* regularly publishes photographs of *dolgozhiteli* who are celebrating their 140th, 150th or 160th birthdays.

An Azerbaijanian gerontologist, Shukur Gasanov, attributes the supposed longevity of his countrymen to their simple ways: "First of all," he says, "they are early risers and they work all the time. Their diet relies mostly on vegetables and milk products — sour milk, kefir, curds and our soft white cheese. They eat many greens and especially fruits like grapes and apricots. And they also fast to rest their stomachs. They drink natural spring water. They stay on the move, and they spend much time in the open air. Even when the weather is cold, they bathe often in

A Georgian "long-lifer" flaunts his fitness by performing a traditional dance. Claims that natives of the Caucasus Mountains enjoy remarkable longevity are often made — and they are just as often disputed.

our cold rivers. They always sleep on hard beds. And not too long — perhaps six hours a night."

The widely touted virtues of these habits in prolonging life have been repeatedly investigated by Westerners (and a few skeptical Russians); the most reliable of these reports indicate that the claims not only seem incredible, they are incredible.

One authority who checked is Dr. Alexander Leaf, Professor of Clinical Medicine at the prestigious Massachusetts General Hospital in Boston. On a visit to the Caucasus in 1975, he was impressed by the health and advanced years of the elderly he saw, and he returned to write a book, *Youth in Old Age*, that generally confirmed the claims of great longevity.

Continuing to follow the cases that he had observed, however, Dr. Leaf became suspicious. One woman who claimed to be 109 years old also told him that she had given birth to a baby when she was 55. Since prolonged fertility was asserted to be one of the manifestations of a long life, Dr. Leaf believed her at first. Then he found out that her baby boy was a stepson. Studying issues of *Pravda*, Dr. Leaf noticed that an obituary of one long-lifer, Shirali Mislimov, was followed in succeeding years by the same picture of Mislimov, congratulating him each time on his birthday. "The last time, he was 170," said a disillusioned Dr. Leaf. He came to the conclusion — as have other investigators — that the claims of remarkable longevity were, at best, exaggerated. "I was gullible," he said.

The tall tales of the long-lifers may have gained credence because the Caucasus is a remote and romantic region. Even more exotic to Europeans are the ways of the peoples living to the east, in the arid lands of Central Asia, which

Uzbek girls show off glossy black hair, coifed into some 40 braids under gold-embroidered caps called *doppi*.

make up nearly 18 per cent of the total area of the U.S.S.R. Here the impact of the Orient is immediately visible in the desert robes of the men, the women who still wear their black, shiny hair in long braids, the felt-covered yurts, or round tents, of the countryside and the ubiquitous teahouses and mosques of the cities.

And yet, even in this faraway eastern land, the signs of transition to the modern world of western Russia are everywhere evident in the clusters of highrise buildings and the sprawling complexes of smoke-spewing factories.

This vast stretch of desert, grasslands and mountains — which reaches from the Caspian Sea all the way to the borders of China — is redolent with the exotic history of trade routes and camel trains, of army outposts and thundering cavalry, of Marco Polo and Genghis Khan. This was the major highway between China and the West, as well as the route of invasion taken by both Cyrus and Alexander. And it was a land of poets and of potentates long before most Slavs were able to read and write. By the 16th Century, however, there was a change: Galleons sailing the Indian Ocean had replaced the caravans; the region lost its profitable trade and slipped into desperate poverty, its people struggling to survive.

Today, Soviet technology — and Russian technicians — have helped transform Central Asia into a productive and populous area. So many Russian settlers have been sent to Kazakhstan to farm in the Virgin Lands Program, for example, that the republic's population, 6.5 million in 1950, more than doubled by 1980; in Alma-Ata, the capital of Kazakhstan, two thirds of the residents are ethnic Russians.

Nevertheless, the influx of Russians has not overwhelmed the descendants of the Tartars. In fact, the opposite may be true. With improved sanitation and health facilities, the Asian birth rate has gone up and is now double that of the Russians. By the year 2000, it may be six times as great. By that time, it is estimated, the Russians' 52 per cent majority in the U.S.S.R. as a whole will have slipped to about a 46 per cent share, and the Central Asians, now accounting for 16 per cent of the total, will make up 21 per cent.

Along the northern reaches of Central Asia, Kazakhstan is home to 200,000 nomadic shepherds, who pack their yurts onto their horses and travel with the seasons, like their ancestors for centuries before them. But many others now are settled farmers, tending newly developed fields that produce a fifth of all the grain that is harvested in the U.S.S.R.

To the southwest, Turkmenistan has been altered in another way. Turkmenistan is desert country: 90 per cent lies in the Kara-Kum desert. Now the Kara-Kum has been made to bloom with cotton, vegetables and alfalfa (for vast herds of Karakul sheep) by a giant canal that cuts through the desert, bringing water down from the Amu Darya river and the Aral Sea all the way to Ashkhabad and Turkmenistan's western border.

The canal, which is 500 miles long, 100 yards wide and 15 feet deep, took eight years to complete. "Our old people had never believed that water could cross the Kara-Kum," said one Turkoman. "When it flowed in, they had to touch it — to dip their hands in it. Some of them began to pray. We feasted for two months."

The snow-capped Pamir mountains rise to the east of Turkmenistan, and in the valleys and on the slopes live the Tadzhiks. Visitors remark on

3

Turkomen in karakul hats, among
the few who still ply the old Silk Road
with camel caravans, rest during
a journey across the Kara-Kum, the
desert that covers 115,000 square
miles in Central Asia.

the handsome men and the beautiful women, with their long black eyelashes and lithe figures. They too have been brought rapidly into the industrial age; Tadzhik cotton fields have the highest yield in the Soviet Union, and Tadzhikistan has a thoroughly modern textile industry.

But many Tadzhiks still prefer the nomadic existence of the goatherd, pursuing with their animals the seasonal supplies of grass and water. Their ancestors' yurts, however, have largely been replaced by modern lightweight tents, equipped with transistor radios blaring Middle Eastern music.

To the north and east is Kirgizia, the U.S.S.R.'s Wild West, a republic of horses and horse-lovers, with a population of about two million of the latter and 265,000 of the former. Horses gallop their way through Kirgiz folklore, and they are still used here for tending sheep in the rocky pasturelands of the mountains, and cattle in the valleys. Horses are also raised for meat — though, says a Kirgiz cowboy, "A Kirgiz would not eat a horse if it had ever been saddled — never!" Horse breeding and cattle raising continue to be important activities, although today they are collectivized.

Modern industry has been introduced to Kirgizia. The region now has sugar-beet farms, textile mills and machinery factories in the valleys, and they are connected to coal mines in the mountains by paved highways.

The most striking examples of the coalescing of old and new can be seen in the heartland of Central Asian culture, Uzbekistan. The home of the Uzbeks

Living in a modern house but sitting, like their nomad ancestors, on a bright Bukhara rug, an Uzbek family shares a meal. The dish is palov — finger food of rice, mutton and vegetables molded into bite-sized balls.

lies exactly athwart the old Silk Road, which once carried trade from the Black Sea in Europe across Central Asia to northwestern China. A narrow trail, it has been worn by countless hooves and wheels until in places it is fully eight feet below the level of the surrounding landscape.

Evidence of Uzbek glory can still be seen, including the mosaic-covered minarets of the great Tamerlane's mausoleum in the ancient capital of Samarkand. Today the structure, partly restored, is surrounded by tall office buildings and apartment houses.

A little more than a hundred miles from Samarkand is the modern Uzbek capital of Tashkent, the largest industrial city in Central Asia. Much of Tashkent was destroyed in 1966 when a series of earthquakes, whose epicenter was directly beneath the city, struck without warning. A modern metropolis has replaced the ancient buildings reduced to rubble by the disaster. Despite the threat of more quakes, subways run under the streets.

In these 20th Century surroundings the Uzbeks continue many of their old ways. In restaurants the background accompaniment often is not music but an elder sitting on a platform reading aloud excerpts from poetry or newspapers, as was the custom in the days when literacy was rare. In open markets independent suppliers, competing with the state stores, haggle with their customers over plate-shaped loaves of bread, red peppers and plums, apples and melons.

When an Uzbek woman comes back home from her factory job at the end of the workday, she is likely to change from her contemporary clothes to her *atlas* (a long loose blouse) and a pair of pantaloons; even though she and her husband may be able to afford a modern stove, she may well prefer to cook her *manty*, *plov* and *lepeski* (dumplings, pilaf and bread) in a stone oven set on the earthen floor of her open kitchen.

The Uzbeks and Kazakhs, Armenians and Azerbaijanians, Lithuanians and Latvians, Ukrainians and Belorussians are major ethnic peoples largely concentrated in major geographical areas. Scattered across the U.S.S.R. are dozens of other smaller groups: Tuvans and Buryats, Udegays, Kets and Komi, Orocks, Aleuts and Ainu. None is more individualistic than the hardy Northern peoples of Siberia, such as the Chukchis.

Most of the aborigines of northwest Siberia were still virtually in the Stone Age at the beginning of the 20th Cen-

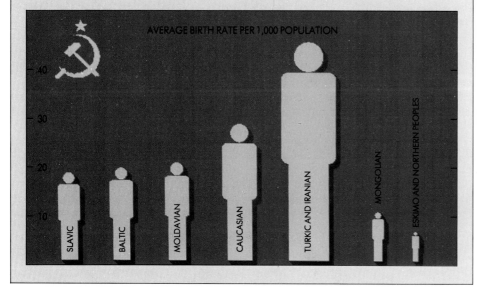

THE RISING POPULATION OF THE EAST

The birth rate among ethnic Russians has been declining, while that of the Soviet Union's Turkic and Iranian peoples of Central Asia has been rising. This increase in births in the eastern U.S.S.R. is due in part to a reduction in infant mortality in the region and in part to the tradition of large families among Muslims.

The Russian birth rate is below the national average of 17.9 per thousand; if the trend continues, the now-dominant Russians will be a minority by the year 2000.

AVERAGE BIRTH RATE PER 1,000 POPULATION

— 40
— 30
— 20
— 10

SLAVIC · BALTIC · MOLDAVIAN · CAUCASIAN · TURKIC AND IRANIAN · MONGOLIAN · ESKIMO AND NORTHERN PEOPLES

tury. Tsarist Russia had done little or nothing to introduce them to modern ways. The Soviet government started with a program of formal education, providing an alphabet — Latin at first but changed to Cyrillic in 1937. Itinerant schoolteachers attempted to follow the nomadic groups as they traveled about the region, but when this proved to be impractical the government intervened and established boarding schools for the children.

As more and more of these children became educated, some of them went on to study in Soviet universities. One of these students was Yuri Rytkheu, a Chukchi who is a popular Soviet novelist. His recollections of his childhood days on Cape Dezhnev, across the Bering Strait from Alaska, evoke the primitive ways of these people of the Soviet Arctic.

"Our whole life was bound up with the sea," Rytkheu writes. "Early in the morning the hunters set off to sea. In winter they hid in the light blue twilight, among the masses of broken ice to hunt seals. In summer the hunters set off into the sparkling patches of sunlight and among the floating icebergs to chase the herds of whales and walruses."

The Chukchis, Rytkheu reports, lived in *yarangi*, portable circular tents that resemble the yurts used by the desert nomads but are covered with walrus hide instead of with felt. Walrus tusks at one time provided the runners for their sleighs and, according to Rytkheu, "the tips of harpoons, handles of knives and numerous other instruments were also fashioned from this strong ivory. Walrus and whale oil burned in stone lamps, warming and illuminating our home. Our entire view of the world, our philosophy, fairy tales, legends and songs were linked with the sea and its animals."

Rytkheu remembers how the 20th Century intruded on this ancient way of life, recalling that the Chukchis saw airplanes before they saw horse-drawn carriages and trains. Soviet commissars came to study the Chukchis as well as educate them, and members of Rytkheu's tribe joked about the "typical family here: father, mother, two children, as well as over there in the corner of the hut, the researcher."

Today's Chukchis have moved into the modern world, some of them even flying from one fishing spot to another by helicopter. They may still live in a *yaranga* but it now is likely to contain recent newspapers and magazines, and at its entranceway waits a radio-equipped snowmobile. The children go off to boarding school in the autumn and return in the spring. Rytkheu himself often returns to his home. The Chukchis, he maintains, still believe that the North, the snows, the cold, the vivid summer tundra and sweet cloudberries make their native land the dearest place on earth.

Some of the Chukchis are reindeer herders as well as whale and walrus hunters. They — and, around the Arctic Circle west to European Lapland, the Evenks, Yakuts and Nenets — continue to pursue this seasonal nomadic occupation, folding their *yarangi* and following the reindeer through the long summer nights while the animals fatten up for the winter.

When, as the Chukchis say, "the moon puts on his furs" in the misty evenings of autumn and the animals move back to their winter grazing grounds, the herders follow along to huddle in their walrus-covered huts through the long months of dark and cold. Reindeer, as Rytkheu points out,

Workers on a collective farm close to the Mongolian border step outside their front door to greet a visitor. The dry steppe is grazing land — mainly for cattle and sheep.

3

are marvelously well adapted to life in this part of the world. They "graze the most meager pastures, and despite all this, they manage by the end of summer to build up enough of a layer of fat to survive the harsh winter."

But in their own nomadic feeding patterns, Arctic reindeer range over wide areas. So when the Soviets tried in the 1930s to collectivize reindeer herding, they found it far more difficult than they had anticipated. For two decades, the government strove to herd the herders into villages. But while the humans could be forced, the reindeer could not; the animals persisted in following their noncollective feeding routes. Faced with the prospect of being left behind without the animals, many of the herders slaughtered all of their reindeer.

Finally, the Soviet authorities realized that they would have to compromise: They collectivized the production and distribution of reindeer meat but allowed the herders to follow their wandering animals. The reindeer herds of the Soviet Arctic, which had declined from two million in 1929 to about half that number in the early 1950s, by the 1980s had recovered to 1.5 million.

Not all ethnic groups have managed to come to terms with the Soviet government as successfully as the reindeer herders. During World War II, several mass deportations took place. The 1.5 million Volga Germans — descendants of settlers who had come to Russia during the 18th Century — were uprooted from their homes in the Volga region and resettled in Central Asia and Siberia. The government feared that they would collaborate with the German invaders. Although there was no evidence of treason, they were also deprived of their civil rights, which were not restored until 1955.

One group of Muslim Tartars, descendants of Bhatu Kahn's Golden Horde, who ruled Russia for two centuries, suffered a similar fate. Next to the Uzbeks, the Tartars are the largest non-Slavic group in the Soviet Union, and nearly every major city in the U.S.S.R. had a Tartar community. However, during World War II, the Tartars who lived in the Crimea were accused of collaborating with the Nazi forces that were occupying their territory. In the course of just a few hours on May 18, 1944, every man, woman and child — some 200,000 in all — was picked up and deported from the Crimea; the great majority of them were sent to Uzbekistan. Their homes were leveled, and all evidence of their existence, including street signs, was obliterated. Like the Volga Germans, they were stripped of their civil rights.

In the 1960s, in an amazingly bold act, 120,000 Crimean Tartars signed a petition asking for their homeland to be returned to them, while 15,000 sent letters and telegrams to government officials. When nothing happened, they got up another petition of 115,000 names and dispatched 20,000

more letters and telegrams. A delegation that was sent to Moscow got arrested, setting off rioting in Uzbekistan. Finally 400 Tartars journeyed to Moscow at the peak of the tourist season and staged a demonstration that had the desired effect: It caught the attention of the foreigners present — and the Kremlin. A month later they were given back their civil rights, though not their Crimean homeland.

In recent years, Moscow has made an attempt to deal with what the Kremlin calls the "nationalities problem" less harshly than Stalin did. Russification is the process by which the Kremlin apparently hopes to be able to keep its diverse and nationalistic ethnic populations under control. While Moscow does encourage the teaching of local languages, it also requires that Russian be the common tongue. Some non-Russians display their resentment of this imposition by deliberately speaking Russian ungrammatically or by affecting comic accents. Still, literacy in the Russian language is increasingly widespread; more than 90 per cent of all Soviet citizens have learned it, for a certain fluency is essen-

From a minaret in Bukhara, Uzbekistan, a muezzin issues a call to prayer. His congregants are among the 30 million Soviet Muslims, most of whom live in Central Asia.

tial to secure and hold a good job.

The practice of ethnic religions is sometimes discouraged and sometimes tolerated. In areas where religious beliefs are deeply ingrained and politically harmless, Moscow tends to permit observance; the Orthodox Church, for example, prospers in the Russian homeland *(pages 108-118)*. In Mongolian border areas, financial support for the once-numerous Buddhist priesthood has been withheld, and few priests remain; however, the old prayer wheels are in common, open use among the faithful. Armenians, who were the first to make Christianity a state religion, continue to hold fast to their faith and observe its traditional practices; Armenian children still flock to the 17-centuries-old Gregorian church in Echmiadzin, leading beribboned farm animals to be blessed before being sacrificed.

The Soviets seem to be more wary of the Muslim religion, knowing that it can be explosively nationalistic. Some 25,000 mosques have been shuttered or leveled in Central Asia, and the number of clerics there has dwindled from 35,000 to 1,000.

Yet with only 300 mosques to serve the 44 million people of the area, traveling mullahs perform the religious rites, and the number of secret Muslim societies has grown rather than declined. "I pray on my own at home," said one staunch believer. "If I were to frequent a mosque, it wouldn't be good for my job." According to a Muslim official in Tashkent, this persistence has brought the total number of Muslims in the U.S.S.R. to 30 million; Moscow puts the figure at two million.

The most persecuted religion of all has been and continues to be that of the Jews. Ironically, after generations of ghettos, pogroms and other, more subtle forms of discrimination, the Russian Jews at first prospered as full-fledged citizens of the Soviet state. The Jewish State Theater was founded in 1919 (the famed painter Marc Chagall was its stage designer); close to 20 other Yiddish-language theater groups sprouted up around the Soviet Union; Yiddish newspapers were published in Moscow and at least three other Soviet cities.

Anti-Semitism returned under Stalin's rule, however: The country's 1,000 Jewish schools were closed, and Jews found themselves discriminated against in jobs. Jews responded by attempting to leave the U.S.S.R., but they were refused exit permits until the 1970s, when some 250,000 of the nation's nearly two million Jews were finally allowed to emigrate.

In repressing or tolerating religions, as in every relationship with this array of ethnic groups, the overriding concern of the dominant Russians is political — the need to control such a vibrant conglomeration of peoples. Each group is ambitious, proud of its past glories, certain of its own superiority and resentful of the Russians' often arrogant oversight.

Tensions between the Russians and their not-quite-equal compatriots are always present and frequently come to the surface. An American graduate student who spent a year among the Uzbeks working on her doctoral thesis recounts one such occurrence in a department store. She asked, in Russian, for laundry detergent and put down a ruble to pay for it. "I only take exact change," announced the clerk. When the American replied that she did not have any change, the clerk shot back: "Then you'll just have to wear dirty underwear."

The woman was amazed. "I looked at him incredulously," she recalled, until finally he responded. " 'Where are you from?' he asked, and when I told him America, he apologized profusely. 'I thought you were Russian,' he said — and then gave me the detergent and my change. I could have been from Europe, China or even another Soviet republic and gotten that detergent. But for Russians in Central Asia, it's very often 'exact change or dirty underwear.' "

An Armenian boy cradles a rooster that will be blessed and sacrificed in thanks for prayers answered.

PEOPLES AT WORK

By law, every citizen of the Soviet Union is entitled to a job. In a country that is so huge and is home to so many diverse ethnic groups, work can take an amazing variety of colorful and distinctive forms, from ballet dancing in Leningrad to herding woolly goats in Central Asia.

Many of these tasks are carried out by native peoples in traditional ways; fruit sellers in the open market in the Muslim city of Tashkent look and work as they have for centuries. But many of their neighbors wear Western-style clothes in textile mills and machine factories, working alongside people who have only recently moved from other regions. Europeans, in particular, have gone east by the thousands to such lightly populated areas as Kazakhstan, to turn steppe into farmland, and to Yakutia, to exploit untapped mineral wealth. The extent of the shuffling of the Soviet peoples can be seen in marriage statistics: 30 per cent of all weddings unite brides and grooms of different ethnic ancestry.

A Moscow model shows off a silver-fox coat. Fashion may not be a Soviet specialty, but furs are. The U.S.S.R. is the world's principal supplier of pelts, most of them from Siberia.

Construction workers take a break at a Moscow building site. Eighty-five per cent of Soviet women hold jobs of some kind.

A Nenets reindeer herder ropes one of the 17,000 animals tended by his collective, near Arkhangelsk. The farm sells 400 tons of reindeer meat a year.

Full of youthful grace, a veteran ballet instructor in a Leningrad school conducts a class.

Smoking a *papirosa* — a cigarette in a cardboard holder — a Ukrainian cowboy keeps his eye on the cattle he tends.

A retired Ukrainian adds to his pension income by turning out combs in his home workshop. Such cottage industries supply many consumer goods.

A Georgian teacher listens to her student practicing the official, standardized lesson.

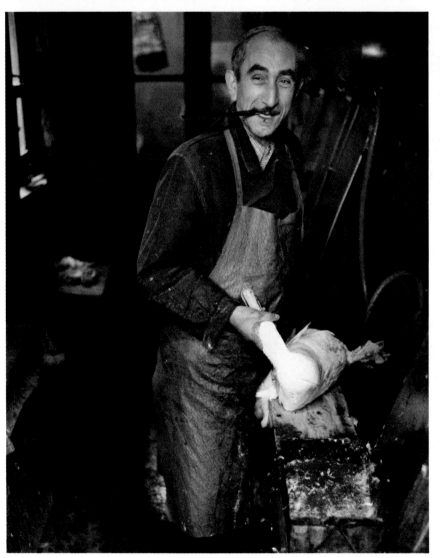

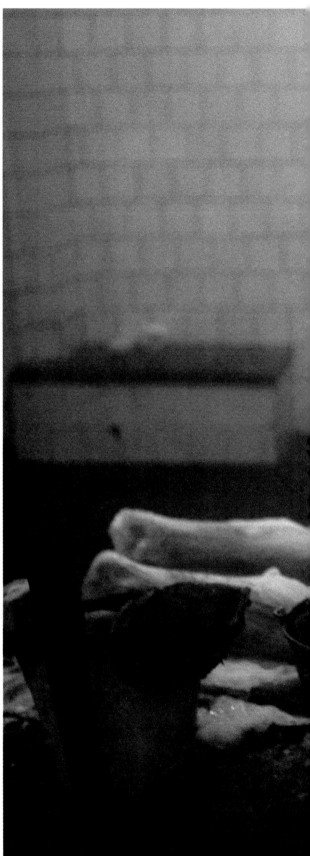

A kosher butcher completes a ritual slaughter in Georgia, home to many Soviet Jews.

86

Shirtless in the steamy atmosphere of a Georgian health spa, a masseur lathers a client for a rubdown.

In Siberia, a European runs a forklift.

A Tashkent street vendor sells pomegranates.

An animal breeder in the Kosh-Agach region of Siberia holds up a young goat, of a type raised for its warm, thick fleece.

Men of the Khevsur tribe, a fierce
Georgian people who claimed descent
from Crusaders, wear medieval
chain mail in this 1890s photograph.
They had been absorbed into the
expanding Russian Empire at the
beginning of the 19th Century.

A LONG AND VIOLENT HISTORY

*She was christened in childhood with a
    lash,
torn to pieces,
        scorched.
Her soul was trampled by the feet,
inflicting blow upon blow,
of Pechenegs,
        Varangians,
            Tartars,
and our own people —
            much more terrible than the Tartars.*

In these few lines from a poem published in 1963, Yevgeni Yevtushenko conveyed the history of Russia and, by extension, the history of the Soviet Union. A land unprotected by natural barriers, it has suffered invasion after invasion — from the east by Pechenegs, Tartars, Khazars and countless others, from the north and west by Varangians, Swedes, Lithuanians, Poles, French and Germans. It has been oppressed by native rulers, who have included some of the cruelest tyrants the world has known. Such a history explains why the Russian people seem so passionately possessive of their land, so distrustful of foreigners, so submissive to authoritarian rule. "Russia's endurance became famous," wrote Yevtushenko. "She did endure."

The story begins in about 1000 B.C. with the Cimmerians, primitive farmers of the plains north of the Black Sea. Around 700 B.C. they were overrun by the first Asiatic horsemen, the Scythians, another long-vanished people,

who left behind in burial mounds a fortune in golden ornaments — diadems, necklaces, bracelets, rings, earrings — that today are national treasures.

The Scythians in turn yielded to a new group of Asiatic nomads, the Sarmatians, and these were followed by the Goths and then the Huns; under their leader, Attila, the Huns went on to terrorize much of Europe, rampaging as far to the west as Orléans, where they were at last defeated by Visigoths and Gallo-Romans in 451 A.D. In the wake of the Huns came the Avars and then the Khazars.

The Khazars were traders, and among the peoples they dealt with were the Slavs, a group of slash-and-burn farmers and fur trappers living in the forested area of present-day Kiev, Novgorod and Moscow. Little is known of their earlier history. Related to other Slavic peoples of Central Europe, these Eastern Slavs waited out the Scythians, Sarmatians, Huns, Avars and other conquerors to become the enduring Russians, a name they acquired in roundabout fashion during the 9th and 10th Centuries.

The name was a Norse gift. Scandinavian traders, the Varangians, using the inland waterways of the Volkov and Dnieper Rivers to reach the rich market of Byzantium, passed right through the Slavic heartland. In time these Norsemen, one group of whom are believed to have been called the Rus, established trading posts in the Slavs' territory.

4

Two of the trading posts, Kiev and Novgorod, grew into fortified towns ruled by Norse princes. And Kiev, strategically located just where the Dnieper breaks out of the forests into the steppe, eventually became the thriving center of the infant Kiev state, the ancestral home of modern Russia.

Around 980, Kiev was under the rule of Vladimir, the first of the long series of autocrats who shaped Russia to their will. By this time most of the rulers of Europe, the Near East and North Africa had adopted one or another of the great monotheistic religions. Europe and Byzantium were governed by Christians, the Arab world by Muslims; to the south of Kiev was the then-independent state of the Khazars, whose rulers had adopted Judaism as their official religion. Vladimir realized that a single state faith could help foster political unity, and he decided that he would impose one, replacing the numerous pagan beliefs then practiced in Russia. According to legend, he decreed the official faith only after sending emissaries to collect information on Islam, Judaism and Christianity.

The first he rejected because it prohibited wine. "Drinking," he said, "is the joy of the Russes." The second he spurned because the originators of Judaism had been forced to flee their homeland, and Vladimir saw no point in adopting the religion of a people who had been dispersed.

That left just the two branches of Christianity. Vladimir's agents, investigating the Roman Catholic Church, "beheld no glory" in it. But in Byzantium they were dazzled by the Eastern Orthodox Church. "The Greeks led us to the buildings where they worshipped their God, and we knew not whether we were in heaven or on earth. For on earth there is no such splendor or such beauty, and we are at a loss to describe it." Impressed by this report, Vladimir arranged to be baptized into the Orthodox Church and forced all of his subjects to do the same.

Vladimir's choice of Eastern Orthodoxy over Western Catholicism had results of lasting significance. It isolated the country from the rest of Europe, provoked abiding suspicion of Western ideas, and incited tragic enmity between Russia and its Roman Catholic neighbors — particularly the Poles.

Vladimir's bold stroke did indeed give the Kiev state a measure of unity. But not for long. Constantly battered by waves of nomadic invaders, it succumbed to the Tartars, who in the 13th Century conquered much of Europe and Asia. The Tartars ruled Russia for more than 200 years, and the fledgling Russian state was reduced to a few small principalities paying tribute to their Tartar masters but tenuously linked by the Orthodox Church.

Kiev, in the midst of the Tartar-held Ukrainian region, was never to regain its political supremacy, although it remains today a principal center of Soviet culture and commerce. Many modern Ukrainians, while claiming credit for the founding of Russia, do not consider themselves Russians. They are, they insist, Ukrainians, and they are a bit scornful of the neighboring Slavs to the north, the Russians who took advantage of the Tartar conquest to gain the power they hold today.

These northern Slavs peopled the principality then known as Muscovy, its chief town a nondescript wooden settlement called Moscow. The Muscovites were only loosely controlled by the Tartars but acknowledged their dominance and paid them tribute. Muscovite princes, cannily using their tribute-paying role to better their own position, collected taxes for their Tartar overlords but then siphoned off some of the take. Eventually they were strong enough to challenge the Tartars.

By a fluke, they were also able to supplant Kiev as the spiritual capital of Russia. The head of the Russian Church, on tour, happened to die in Moscow, and the Muscovite princes seized the opportunity to persuade his successor to transfer his seat from Kiev to Moscow. Thus fortified with temporal and spiritual power, Muscovy finally threw off Tartar rule in 1380, and by 1462 a potent Moscow prince, Ivan III, asserted his authority over Novgorod and Kiev as well as Moscow, uniting the Slavic principalities into the Russian nation. Ivan took to calling himself Tsar — the Russian equivalent of Caesar, which was the title of the Emperors of Rome. His contemporaries referred to him as Ivan the Great.

Although Ivan III was an autocrat,

he ruled with an even hand. The same cannot be said about his grandson, Ivan IV, whose rule was so tyrannical that he is remembered as Ivan the Terrible. The Russian word *"grozny,"* which is translated as "terrible," actually means "awesome," and indeed there was a kind of grandeur in Ivan's excesses. Toward the end of his 51-year reign, which was the longest in Russian history, he was surely mad.

There was much in Ivan's childhood to account for such an end. At three, he lost his father; at eight, his mother died under mysterious circumstances, presumably poisoned. Members of two boyar, or noble, families, the Bielskys and Shuiskys, seized power as his regents. In public they accorded him respect, but in private they treated him, in his own words, "as a menial," denying him food and clothes while they ransacked the imperial treasury. Murders, executions and unexplained imprisonments were commonplace occurrences. One night the boy Ivan was awakened by soldiers who burst into his bedroom looking for a priest they had been ordered to kill.

Ivan took part in formal state affairs from the age of five, and when he was 13 years old, he donned the official robes of the Tsar and presided over meetings of the Bielsky and Shuisky regents. In that role, he proved anything but pliable. At one meeting he delivered a routine criticism of mismanagement and waste; then, taking advantage of bickering among the regents, he did something utterly unexpected: He singled out one regent, Andrei Shuisky, and ordered him arrested. When the astonished Shuisky tried to escape, he was clubbed to death by palace dog-keepers, whom the young Ivan had befriended. Ivan had not intended

Ivan IV, the Terrible, whose benign expression in this 16th Century portrait belies his murderous cruelty, may himself have been murdered. Soviet scientists examining his remains found traces of poison.

Shuisky's death, only his capture, but the boy took responsibility for the murder and indeed capitalized on it, gathering more and more autocratic power to himself.

When he was 16, Ivan was crowned Tsar in a ceremony that he planned for maximum pomp. Three times he was showered with gold and silver coins, to symbolize the prosperity that would distinguish his reign. Bells pealed throughout the country. Three weeks afterward he was married to Anastasia Zakharina-Romanov, a member of a titled family that was subsequently to play a central role in Russian history. Anastasia was beautiful and intelligent, and Ivan adored her.

Many historians divide Ivan's reign into a good half and a bad half. Ivan took all real power away from the boyars and governed singlehandedly and dictatorially. However, in the first years of his rule, the benign and progressive half, he called a general assembly made up of boyars from many noble families and issued edicts based on their advice. He required this hereditary aristocracy to supply soldiers to the Army, easing a burden that had been borne entirely by the landed gentry. A

learned man himself, he ordered rare manuscripts to be imported, established presses to publish books, and set scholars to work translating Russian manuscripts into other languages to show the world that Russia was not backward. And he recommended that music — one of his abiding passions — be taught in all schools.

Ivan simultaneously pressed against the Tartars still controlling Russian lands and sent his troops to conquer other peoples, beginning the expansion of the Empire. In 1555, to celebrate the final rout of the Tartars in Kazan, he caused a great church to be built in Moscow's Red Square, the extravagantly ornate St. Basil's. Actually a cluster of nine chapels forming an eight-pointed star, it is topped by fancifully carved steeples and domes of different heights and colors, all of them based on the wooden architecture of traditional churches, although in fact they are masonry.

Ivan's grandiose gestures extended even to the table. He thought nothing of presiding over five- and six-hour banquets for hundreds, even thousands, of guests, each of whom he greeted on arrival by name. Dinner on such occasions was served on gem-encrusted gold and silver plates, and guests drank from carnelian goblets or from reindeer horns and ostrich eggshells. The food was similarly lavish. Roast swan might be followed by roast peacock, goose with millet, spiced crane and sturgeon. Between courses the servants changed livery, and Ivan himself often changed crowns.

In 1560, Anastasia died mysteriously, and the bad half of Ivan's reign began. He was convinced the Tsarina had been poisoned. His mind seemed to shatter, and he sank into a life of dissi-

Where the Kremlin now stands, wooden walls enclose all of 12th Century Moscow, founded by Prince Yuri Dolgoruky. It was then a wilderness settlement on the Moskva River route south to the Caspian Sea.

A roast swan in full plumage
is brought to lavishly dressed guests
toasting a bashful bride in this 19th
Century painting. Such extravagant
feasts were a tradition of the
Russian aristocracy; one given by Ivan
the Terrible lasted three days.

pation and paranoia. Anyone whom he even remotely suspected of plotting against him was executed, and in 1570 he ordered thousands of citizens of Novgorod killed when civil unrest disturbed that city.

To protect himself against "traitors," Ivan established a personal security force, the *oprichnina* — the first of Russia's infamous secret-police forces. Dressed in black and riding coal-black horses, this band of men, eventually 6,000 strong, rode the countryside to find and destroy anyone suspected of disloyalty to Ivan. Whole towns were wiped out and even a cousin of the Tsar was murdered, along with his family. Then, in another fateful move late in his reign, Ivan took to exiling his political opponents to newly conquered lands in Siberia.

Banishment to Siberia may have been better than the punishment dealt out in Moscow, where Ivan's supposed enemies were likely to be tortured sadistically. Ivan personally took part. When he was particularly angry, said an observer, he foamed at the mouth like a wild horse. During one violent episode, he struck and killed his eldest son, whom he professed to love. This deed pushed Ivan over the brink. He became obsessed with knowing when he himself would die, and in 1584 he sent for 60 witches from Lapland, who obliged him by specifying a date. His death would come, they said, on March 18 of that same year. On March 17, Ivan suffered a seizure and within minutes was "stark dead," as Sir Jerome Horsey, the English Ambassador to Ivan's court, put it.

Ivan's death began a generation of chaos, called the Time of Troubles, that was marked by dynastic struggles, social upheaval and foreign intrusion.

Ivan's weak, incompetent son Feodor inherited the throne, but power was held by Feodor's brother-in-law, Boris Godunov (subject of the opera of that name), who is said to have reinforced his position by killing Feodor's younger brother, Dmitri. Boris was eventually crowned Tsar, but there followed one of the most bizarre episodes in all history: Two different pretenders claimed in succession to be the murdered Dmitri, supposedly still alive.

The two false Dmitris were sponsored by Poland, which had long contested the ownership of Russia's western lands and which during the Time of Troubles repeatedly invaded the country and even occupied Moscow.

Alarmed by the threat of a Polish takeover, a special assembly sought a Tsar who could rally the country's factions and preserve Russian independence. In 1613 the crown was offered to Mikhail Romanov, a prince whose family connection to Ivan's Anastasia gave him great respectability. Mikhail fought off the Poles, stabilized the government and established a dynasty that was to last three centuries, until the 1917 Revolution.

The early Romanovs were undistinguished rulers, but at the close of the 17th Century that dynasty gave Russia a Tsar who was as powerful as Ivan the Terrible, yet without Ivan's destructiveness. He was Peter the Great, the architect of modern Russia.

Like Ivan, Peter suffered a traumatic childhood. His father died when he was 10, and the boy was named co-Tsar, forced by court politics to share the title with a mentally retarded half-brother. He grew up an eyewitness to vicious power struggles and even murders in the corridors of the Kremlin: He once saw a close family friend

Tsar Peter the Great, towering over his retinue in this 1907 painting, strides over the marshy site of his future capital and "window on the West," named St. Petersburg after his patron saint — today the city of Leningrad.

dragged from a hiding place and killed.

But Peter was frequently able to escape to the imperial estate outside Moscow. There he led a remarkably free existence, roaming the countryside by himself and wandering through the local village. By watching and helping, he acquired an astonishing set of skills. Although his talents may have been exaggerated in contemporary accounts, he reportedly could build a masonry house, cobble shoes, pull teeth, even cast a cannon.

According to one story, the young Peter came upon a sailboat in the imperial storehouse and was struck by its unusual design. Unlike the flat-bottomed craft that plied Russian rivers, this one was a round-bottomed sailboat, with a pointed prow and a keel. Peter put it in the water and found a Dutch-born boat builder to teach him how to sail it. From this experience may have come Peter's lifelong love of sailboats and the sea, a passion that would eventually lead him to establish the Russian Navy.

In 1696, when Peter was 24, his half-brother died and Peter became sole ruler. By this time he was a giant of a man, 6 feet 8 inches tall and of legendary strength. It was said that he could bend heavy silver plates as if they were paper and could fell a tree with an ax in seconds. His appetite for food and drink was gargantuan, and he preferred to indulge it in the easy company of for-

eign craftsmen — English, Scottish, Swiss and Danish — living in Moscow. At court, he hugely enjoyed telling coarse jokes that offended many of his listeners.

Peter saw that Russia was backward socially and technologically, and he determined to "open a window to the West" for progressive European ideas. Accordingly, he set forth in 1697 for an epochal tour of Europe.

Peter was traveling incognito, as "Seaman Peter Mikhailov." But this pose was less than successful, since the "seaman" had a retinue of about 270 people. His journey, which lasted for 18 months, took him to Germany, then down the Rhine River to Holland, where he lived and worked for three months as a carpenter in a shipyard, earning a shipbuilder's certificate. Elsewhere, he studied anatomy and surgery by watching a dissection, explored museums and art galleries, and learned how to cut up whale blubber. In England, he observed Parliament from the upper galleries.

The English government billeted him in a nobleman's house. This he left in such disarray — its furniture broken, its portraits used for target practice — that the owner submitted a bill for damages. According to one story, Peter paid up by handing the man a huge uncut diamond wrapped in a piece of dirty paper.

Peter planned to visit Venice next, but his trip was cut short by news of a palace revolt. In his absence, conservative officers of the Streltsy Guard, fearful of his innovative ideas, sought to depose him. Peter rushed home in a fury, only to find that the uprising had already been put down, with hundreds of the rebels killed and more than a thousand thrown in jail. But Peter was not satisfied. He had the prisoners roasted alive on a spit, one by one. As each neared death, his head was lopped off (Peter himself reputedly participated in this grisly finale). Then he had the heads impaled and placed throughout Moscow, to rot.

For all his barbaric behavior, Peter continued to believe that Russia should be modernized. He began symbolically, compelling Russians to adopt the Western styles of dress he had observed in Europe. Men were ordered to shave their beards or else pay a tax; Peter even assisted in the barbering of some noblemen. Short coats were to be substituted for the long Russian caftan; women were to shed their veils and attend parties in the tight-waisted, deeply cut gowns worn by French ladies.

His other reforms were more practical. He encouraged the construction of factories, founded schools of mathematics, navigation, astronomy, medicine, philosophy, geography and politics. He started the first Russian newspaper, ordered the printing of 600 books and built a theater in Moscow on Red Square.

He modernized the Army to enable it to cope with continuing foreign invasions. After Russia lost 10,000 men and most of its artillery against a much smaller Swedish force in the Battle of Narva in 1700, Peter rebuilt his Army in a single year. He instituted new standards of discipline, ordered training for battle rather than for parade-ground maneuvers, and armed his troops with English-made flintlocks to replace the swords, lances and halberds they had previously carried. He even ordered church bells melted down to cast new artillery.

Eight years later the Swedes, who had postponed further conquests of Russia while invading Poland and Saxony, returned. They moved into the Ukraine and there, in 1709, were destroyed in what is considered one of history's most critical encounters, the Battle of Poltava. Sweden was forced to give Russia its lands on the eastern shore of the Baltic — the European mainland — and the threat of Swedish domination of Northern Europe was permanently ended.

After this victory Peter continued to refine his Army; he also brought the Church under state control and reorganized the civil service, setting up 14 grades, to which anyone could aspire. Even a peasant, properly schooled, could rise from the 14th grade to the first. Moreover, every civil servant above the 11th grade automatically became a member of the gentry, gaining the right to own land and serfs; above the eighth grade, such status became hereditary. Traveling this egalitarian route to advancement, Ilya Ulianov, son of a serf and father of the 20th Century revolutionary known as Lenin, climbed the ladder to the fourth grade, becoming a hereditary member of the gentry. Thus Lenin himself was technically an aristocrat.

With the final victory over Sweden, Peter at last acquired his "window on the West," a safe, year-round route through the Baltic Sea to the rest of Europe. In expectation, he had already begun to build a port, the city now called Leningrad but originally named for Peter's patron saint, and thus in a way for Peter himself: St. Petersburg. It would seem to have been set on the worst possible spot — marshland at the mouth of the Neva River, where it flows into the Gulf of Finland.

Peter imported a multitude of French and Italian architects and artisans and proceeded at top speed. Tens of thousands of peasants, prisoners of war and Army recruits were dragooned for labor. Often they dug with their hands, slept in the open and drank stagnant marsh water. So many died that the city was said to have been built on bones. In nine years, however, Peter had his great city — a metropolis of thousands of buildings. He proclaimed it Russia's capital.

Peter's plan for his city included a network of canals, like those of Amsterdam, and broad, tree-lined streets. Houses were sized according to the status of their occupants. Common people were to have one-story houses with four windows and a dormer; prosperous merchants, two-story houses with dormers and a balcony.

Peter's own palace was a modest wood building next to the naval headquarters, where he often took his meals, dining on rations of smoked beef and beer. However, his suburban Summer Palace on the banks of the Neva River, Petrodvoretz (also called Peterhof, a German name), was a 14-room mansion surrounded by elaborate gardens and spectacular fountains. Some of these waterworks catered to Peter's delight in practical jokes: "Surprise" fountains sprayed water on the unwary when they happened to step on a particular stone.

It was at Petrodvoretz that the Tsar had a tragic confrontation with his only living son. Alexis had been born to Peter's first wife, a woman he never liked; eventually he banished her to a convent, in effect divorcing her. His second wife, with whom he lived for 23 years, was a commoner. They had 12 children, but only two survived childhood. Both were girls.

Alexis, the logical successor, was the

4

pawn of conservatives who wanted to depose Peter. At Petrodvoretz, the Tsar accused his son of joining in a plot against him. When Alexis answered him equivocally, Peter had him imprisoned and "questioned" so severely that Alexis died. Peter himself died only seven years later, without ever naming a successor. His death was caused by an illness he contracted when he jumped into the icy water of the Gulf of Finland to help rescue a boatload of foundering sailors.

Peter's modernization was beneficial in many respects, but it also proved divisive. It created a Western-oriented gentry at odds with a peasantry and clergy that violently resisted change from old Russian ways. Barely a half century later, another strong leader widened this chasm. Catherine the Great at first welcomed liberal Western ideas and instituted additional reforms. By the middle of her reign, however, she reversed herself, setting the country on a reactionary course that inexorably led, a century and a half later, to revolution.

Catherine was not even Russian, and "Catherine" was not her real name. She became ruler of Russia through a convoluted series of events set off when Peter the Great died with the imperial succession unsettled. The crown then passed among members of his family, coming to rest in 1741 on his daughter Elizabeth. Elizabeth named as her successor a nephew, a German prince, Peter of Holstein. She also selected a wife for Peter, a minor German princess, Sophie of Anhalt-Zerbst, who later adopted the appropriately Russian name of Catherine.

Clever and anxious to please, with a will of iron and energy to match, Catherine set out to learn her new language and to become an expert on everything Russian. She also soon ignored her young husband, who drank heavily and was thoroughly disagreeable. Six months after his accession to the throne, Catherine engineered a coup that deposed him; then she had herself named Empress of Russia.

Ten days later Peter was conveniently killed, allegedly in a drunken brawl, very likely at Catherine's instigation. "Little Mother, he is no more," wrote one of his companions to her. "Sovereign lady, the mischief is done."

The coup that eliminated Peter was carried out by a handsome young officer of the palace guards, Gregory Orlov, who was one of Catherine's many lovers. She was to have at least 21, and she never made much attempt to hide them. Catherine was not pretty, but she was witty and passionate, and she treated her favorites handsomely. One, Stanislaw Poniatowski, she made King of Poland.

Although Catherine craved power and worked hard to achieve it, she also enjoyed the trappings of majesty. For her coronation she ordered a crown containing almost 5,000 diamonds, 76 perfectly matched pearls and a 399-carat spinel that had once belonged to a Manchu Emperor of China. Thereafter the official headdress for all coronations, this crown was so heavy that one Tsar complained that wearing it gave him a headache.

She also spent millions of rubles on palaces and country estates, and she changed St. Petersburg from a city of wooden structures into an imposing one of granite. She enlarged and elaborated on Peter's city palace and next to it built a gallery, called the Hermitage, to house her library and art collection, filling it with the greatest masterpieces her agents could find — Rembrandts, Raphaels, Van Dykes and Rubenses, among others. Ultimately her collection contained some 4,000 paintings by Europe's finest artists.

This relentlessly intellectual woman, the possessor of a mind that she described as "more masculine than feminine," became fascinated with the ideas of the Enlightenment. This liberal philosophy, which was then sweeping Europe and America, held that human beings were basically good, rather than sinful (as Christian theologians have maintained). One of its fundamental principles held all people to be endowed with rights that no government could override.

Although such views hardly accorded with Russian tradition, Catherine carried on a brisk correspondence with such Enlightenment figures as Voltaire and Diderot. Diderot traveled to St. Petersburg to call on Catherine, but the visit did not go well. The Frenchman took liberties, tapping the Tsarina on the knee and calling her "my good woman." Catherine was not amused.

Under the influence of the Enlightenment, Catherine drew up a new code of laws, based on the premise that a monarch ruled not by the will of God but by the dictates of human reason — a significant difference. She also seemed ready to take up the Enlightenment principle of opposition to human bondage, which had persisted in Russia — even increased there — after it had declined in Europe.

By the 18th Century, slavery was essentially gone in Western Europe, and serfdom, the medieval system that bound peasants to the land of a feudal lord, was about to disappear. But in Russia, serfdom expanded as Tsars repaid favors with gifts of land — along with the peasants living on the land, who thus became serfs of the new landowner. By Catherine's time, approximately half the total population of Russia were serfs, many of them living under conditions tantamount to slavery. One noblewoman in Catherine's court kept her hairdresser, who was a serf, in a cage so that he could not tell anyone that she was bald.

Any possibility that Catherine might free the serfs was foreclosed by an unexpected threat to her power: In the midst of a war with Turkey over the Crimea, Catherine was faced with a peasant rebellion in the Cossack homeland west of the Ural Mountains.

The uprising was led by a black-bearded Cossack named Pugachev, an Army deserter who had persuaded other Cossacks to organize against the St. Petersburg government. Soon the Cossacks, fierce fighters who made up the mounted troops guarding the frontiers, were joined by other dissidents — serfs, miners, conservative monks and political exiles. Pugachev attracted some of his followers by claiming that he was the true Tsar, Catherine's late husband Peter, not dead after all. To convince doubters, he showed them the "Tsar's sign," a scar on his chest. Others he won over by promising them land of their own.

By 1773, Pugachev had attracted some 15,000 adherents, and he controlled large areas of eastern Russia. When he showed an inclination to move on Moscow, Catherine quickly concluded a peace with Turkey and sent part of her Army to capture him. He was brought to Moscow in a cage, and there he was beheaded and quartered. During the months that followed, peasants in every village involved in the rebellion were hanged,

Though known for her extravagance, Catherine the Great was a hard-working Empress. She rose at five in the morning and spent 10 to 15 hours a day reading state papers and working on legislation.

and serfdom, far from being abolished, was extended. New laws made serfs of all the peasants then farming the rich lands of the Ukraine, where serfdom had been rare.

Catherine turned against the Enlightenment. She banned Voltaire's writings and attacked his ideas. As the years passed, she became more and more autocratic. But if her opinions changed, her life style did not. To her legion of lovers she added the most remarkable of them all, the tall, dashing Gregory Potemkin, a well-educated Guardsman 10 years her junior.

When he was introduced to her at a party at the home of her earlier lover, Orlov, Potemkin had the impudence to

"The richest object that ever existed in Europe," Catherine the Great's jeweler said of the coronation crown he made for her. It holds 4,936 diamonds and a 399-carat spinel — alone worth "a load of golden ingots."

parody her German-accented Russian. The other guests were appalled, but Catherine laughed. A tempestuous love affair followed. Catherine delighted in Potemkin's knowledge of Greek and Latin, French and German, and she showered him with endearments, calling him "my peacock," "my Cossack," "my golden pheasant." According to rumor, impossible to confirm, they were secretly married.

Although their ardor cooled after two years, Potemkin remained Catherine's closest friend and adviser; he selected all her subsequent lovers. He was rich in his own right, with luxurious tastes (he bathed in a silver bathtub and passed out diamonds to women at his dinner parties). Catherine made him richer. She presented him with several estates and built a magnificent palace for him in St. Petersburg.

Potemkin, for his part, served her well. He masterminded Russia's annexation of the Crimea in 1783, afterward arranging for Catherine to make an impressive inspection trip through the area. As the guests floated down the Dnieper River on red-and-gold Roman galleys, he pointed out newly built, prosperous towns. This display of progress has been considered a fake, contrived to fool Catherine — giving rise to the expression "Potemkin villages," referring to any elaborate sham — but recent research has convinced many historians that the villages and the progress they represented were, in fact, genuine.

When Potemkin died of malaria in 1791, Catherine was desolated. She died five years later, leaving behind an enlarged country that was improved by her innovations — such as the enlightened code of law and her magnificent art collection — but divided and impov-

1000-700 B.C. Along the northern shore of the Black Sea, a primitive farming culture flourishes among a Slavic people called Cimmerians. They herd animals, weave cloth and produce fine pottery.

500 B.C. Tribes of Slavic peoples from northern Europe live in the region stretching from the marshes of Poland east and south to the Don River.

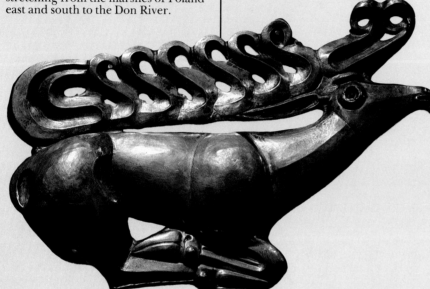

700-300 B.C. The Scythians, nomadic horsemen from Central Asia, take control from the Cimmerians and Slavs and hold sway over grasslands from the Danube to the Don River and across the Caucasus Mountains into Asia Minor. Skilled metalworkers, the Scythians make lavish jewelry, weapons and utensils out of gold *(above)*.

300 B.C.-200 A.D. Iranian-speaking nomads, the Sarmatians, defeat the Scythians and establish the west-east trade route — reaching to the Baltic and Black Seas and beyond — that introduces Graeco-Iranian culture and eventually enriches Russia.

200-370 A.D. The Goths, Germanic invaders from the Baltic area, take over the Sarmatian domain, penetrating into the Crimea in 362.

370-658 The Goths move on to other regions in Europe and Asia, pushed out by Asiatic invaders. These Eastern horsemen — including the Huns led by Attila and, later, the Avars — do not settle but sweep across the sparsely populated regions to the south.

c. 658-900 The Khazars, a tribe of Asian traders, establish their rule in the lower Volga and the southeastern Russian steppe. They build strong commercial ties with the Slavs to the northwest near the Baltic end of the trade route.

862 The Varangians, led by Rurik the Viking, settle Novgorod, in the northern part of Russia. One group is believed to have been called the Rus.

882-912 Prince Oleg *(below)* moves southward to seize control of Slavic communities from the Khazars and makes Kiev the capital of the first truly Russian state.

980-1015 Vladimir, Grand Prince of Kiev, adopts the Christian faith of the Byzantine Church and establishes the Russian Orthodox Church.

1019-1054 Kievan Russia reaches its zenith under Yaroslav the Wise, who promotes education, codifies law, supports the arts, builds cathedrals, and cements alliances with foreign states. His death in 1054 ushers in a period of decline.

1237-1240 The Tartars (or Mongols), already conquerors of much of Asia, sack Kiev in 1240 and inaugurate more than two centuries of control by Tartar overlords, or khans, ruling through Russian vassals.

1240-1242 Alexander Nevsky, Prince of Novgorod, repels invasions from the northwest by Sweden and the Teutonic Knights.

1328-1340 Ivan I, Prince of Moscow, expands his territory and becomes the Tartars' principal vassal. He arranges for Moscow to replace Kiev as the spiritual capital of Russia.

1462-1505 Ivan III *(above)* — also known as Ivan the Great — renounces Tartar rule and establishes the independent Russian state.

1547-1560 Ivan IV — Ivan the Terrible — is crowned Tsar, the first Russian ruler to assume the title officially. He drives the Tartars from their remaining territories along the trade route to the Caspian Sea. He marries Anastasia Zakharina-Romanov, daughter of a powerful Russian family. Under her beneficent influence, he calls the first general assembly to advise him, orders the printing of books and builds St. Basil's Cathedral to commemorate the defeat of the Tartars.

1560-1584 Anastasia Romanov mysteriously dies and Ivan IV turns to irrational repression. He sets up a secret security force, the *oprichnina (above)*, and, suspecting treason, razes Novgorod, killing and torturing thousands. In 1583, Cossack troops conquer Siberia, extending Russian rule into Asia.

1598-1612 Boris Godunov, regent for Ivan's weak son, Feodor, becomes Tsar; this begins the "Time of Troubles." Pretenders claiming to be Ivan's murdered heir, Dmitri, seek the crown; one false Dmitri, backed by Poland, rules briefly. The Poles occupy and burn Moscow in 1610.

1612-1682 Prince Dmitri Pozharski, leading an army raised by a patriot, Kuzma Minin, drives the Poles from Moscow. A year later the general assembly elects Mikhail Romanov Tsar, establishing the dynasty that rules until 1918. Mikhail's successors take the eastern Ukraine from Poland, and extend Russian influence in Siberia to the Pacific. Serfdom is established.

1682-1725 Peter the Great *(symbolized by his ax, below)* becomes Tsar and attempts to modernize the country. He builds a navy, reorganizes the Army and in 1696 tours Europe to gather Western ideas. Peter wages wars against Sweden, winning lands on the Baltic after the decisive Battle of Poltava in 1709. St. Petersburg is built and declared the capital.

1762-1796 Catherine II — Catherine the Great — begins as a progressive and benevolent ruler but reverses liberalization after a vast peasant revolt in 1773. Her interference in the affairs of Poland leads to the partition of that country and to war with Turkey. Russia gains the Crimea, Lithuania, much of the Ukraine. Fur traders establish settlements in Alaska in 1784.

1801-1812 Russia expands further, annexing Georgia and, in 1809, Finland. Scattered Russian settlements are established along the west coast of North America as far south as California; Tsar Alexander I orders forts built in Alaska. In 1812, Napoleon Bonaparte invades Russia and sacks Moscow *(below)*, but his army is repulsed and nearly annihilated. This victory makes Russia a leading power in Europe.

1861-1876 Tsar Alexander II liberates the serfs *(above)*. Russia sells Alaska to the United States in 1867.

1898-1903 The Social Democratic Party is formed and splits in 1903 into two factions: the moderate Mensheviks, and the extremist Bolsheviks, led by Vladimir Ulianov, called Lenin.

1904-1905 Russia occupies Manchuria and attempts to penetrate China and Korea, leading to the Russo-Japanese War and a humiliating defeat at the hands of the Japanese. Growing unrest spurs strikes and demonstrations; hundreds of men, women and children are killed on "Bloody Sunday," when police open fire on protesting workers. Yielding to pressure for reform, Tsar Nicholas II issues the October Manifesto, establishing the Duma, an elected assembly.

1825-1856 Young Army officers, calling for Constitutional reforms and an end to serfdom, lead the Decembrist Revolt in St. Petersburg. The uprising is violently suppressed. Russia is defeated by Britain, France and Turkey in the Crimean War (1853-1856).

1914-1917 Germany declares war on Russia. Major defeats lead Tsar Nicholas II to go to the front, leaving Tsarina Alexandra in charge in the capital. But the government is dominated by her adviser, the monk Rasputin, who is assassinated in 1916.

1917-1918 A troop mutiny in the capital brings about the collapse of the monarchy. The Duma sets up a provisional government; Alexander Kerensky becomes Premier. Political instability leads to a second uprising, the October Revolution: Bolsheviks, led by Lenin *(above, center)*, Leon Trotsky *(above, right)* and cohorts such as Josef Stalin *(above, left)* seize power and in 1918 sign a peace treaty with Germany.

1918 Civil war breaks out between the Bolsheviks and the anti-Communist White Army *(above)*. The Tsar and his family are executed.

1921 The White Army is defeated, and Lenin consolidates the power of the Communists.

1922 Josef Stalin becomes General Secretary of the Communist Party, and the Union of Soviet Socialist Republics is officially established.

1924-1929 Lenin dies, leading to a struggle for power between Stalin and Trotsky; Stalin wins and Trotsky is exiled. Intensive collectivization of farms and rapid industrialization begin.

1936-1938 Stalin undertakes the Great Purge. Millions whom he suspects of opposing him — including many scientists, artists and writers as well as 200 of the top military commanders — are arrested and exiled or executed.

1939-1945 The U.S.S.R. and Germany agree to carve up Poland between them, but in 1941 Germany invades the Soviet Union, reaching Moscow's suburbs. After huge losses of territory and lives — 20 million killed — Soviet armies defeat the German forces and occupy much of Eastern Europe. At the Yalta Conference, Franklin D. Roosevelt and Winston Churchill tacitly grant Stalin a "sphere of influence" in Europe, giving the U.S.S.R. effective control over Rumania, Bulgaria, Poland, Hungary, Czechoslovakia, Yugoslavia, Albania and East Germany.

1947-1950 The Cold War begins. A treaty of mutual assistance is concluded with the People's Republic of China. The U.S.S.R. explodes its first atomic bomb.

1953-1956 Stalin dies; Nikita Khrushchev *(below)* takes over, denounces Stalin, and brings some liberalization. He crushes a revolt in Hungary.

1957 An intercontinental ballistic missile is successfully tested and *Sputnik I*, the first space satellite, is launched.

1960-1965 China and the Soviet Union spar openly, marking the start of the Sino-Soviet split. The Soviets launch the first manned space flight, leading to the first space walk *(above)*.

1964-1965 Khrushchev is ousted, to be replaced by Leonid I. Brezhnev *(below)*. In a revitalized economy, emphasis is placed on increasing the production of consumer goods.

1968 The Soviet government sends troops into Czechoslovakia.

1972 U.S. President Richard Nixon visits Moscow and signs the first Strategic Arms Limitation Treaty (SALT I), a keystone of détente between the U.S. and the Soviet Union.

1979 The Soviets invade Afghanistan in an effort to crush an anti-Marxist Muslim rebellion. Fierce resistance by the Afghan guerrillas drains Soviet resources and manpower.

1980 Soviet interference in Poland suppresses liberal activities of Solidarity, the coalition of labor unions.

1982 Leonid Brezhnev dies and is replaced by Yuri Andropov, former chief of the Soviet Committee for State Security — the KGB.

1983 Yuri Andropov dies and is replaced by Konstantin Chernenko.

1985 For the third time in 28 months, a Soviet leader dies: Mikhail Gorbachev succeeds Chernenko.

erished by her many extravagances.

Less than 20 years after Catherine's death, the country suffered the first of a series of disastrous events that were to plague it through the 19th Century and into the 20th. Napoleon Bonaparte, representing the culture Catherine had once praised, invaded the country and occupied Moscow, although the severe Russian winter soon forced him to retreat. In December 1825, an even more ominous event took place. Liberal-minded Army officers led soldiers to demonstrate in St. Petersburg for financial reforms, a constitutional monarchy and an end to serfdom. The Decembrist Revolt, as it came to be called, was quickly snuffed out, and five leaders were hanged.

Many of the changes the reformers had asked for, including the abolition of serfdom, were made two generations later by a more moderate Tsar, Alexander II. But in 1881 Alexander was assassinated by a bomb thrown under his carriage by student revolutionaries (they had made six previous attempts to kill him). Terrorist activity continued, and assassinations occurred with frightening frequency; in the single year of 1906, a total of 768 officials were killed.

The government was buffeted from within and without. In 1905, a humiliating defeat in a war with the small nation of Japan destroyed most of the antiquated Russian fleet. Then, a workers' demonstration grew into a march by thousands of workers and their families to the Winter Palace. The Tsar, Nicholas II, a gentle but ineffectual man, was not at home. In his absence, his guards opened fire on the crowd, killing some 500 men, women and children.

Bloody Sunday, as it is called, out-raged the Russian people. Resentment flared against the Tsar himself, who, up to that point, had escaped direct blame for the country's troubles. An alarmed Nicholas hastily granted one of his people's demands: He convened an elected assembly, called the Duma, but it lacked meaningful power.

World War I was the final disaster for the monarchy. The Romanov regime —a political anachronism, trying to run a 20th Century nation like an 18th Century agrarian state — was completely unprepared. Six weeks after war had been declared on Germany, Russian generals were already complaining of a shortage of artillery ammunition, and were rationing some units to five shells a day. After mobilizing six million men, the government discovered it had only five million rifles.

In 1915, with Russian armies retreating everywhere and casualties in the millions, Nicholas left St. Petersburg to take personal command of the armed forces. In charge at home was Tsarina Alexandra, who relied on advice from an illiterate "holy man," Gregory Rasputin. Years before, Rasputin had allegedly stopped the hemorrhaging of the Tsar's hemophiliac son; ever since, his word had been law to the Tsarina, even though he was a coarse peasant, a drunk and a lecher. "My much loved, never to be forgotten teacher, savior and instructor," she wrote to him, "my soul is only rested and at ease when you are near me."

Rasputin's influence was calamitous, and in December 1916 a group of noblemen decided to do away with him. But the monk was not easy to kill. First they fed him cream cakes laced with cyanide. When that had no effect, one of the assassins shot him. Rasputin dropped to the floor but then leaped

Gregory Rasputin, the Siberian holy man who mesmerized Tsarina Alexandra and became a power behind the throne, sits with two women of the court. His baleful influence contributed to Nicholas' downfall.

up and tried to strangle his assailant. Finally one of the conspirators pumped bullets into him until he fell, and the conspirators then made absolutely sure of his death by dumping his body into the Neva River.

This tragic farce was but one of many events presaging collapse of the Empire. All through February and early March of 1917, mobs of striking workers roamed the streets of the capital— which had now been renamed Petrograd. On March 11, soldiers at the Petrograd garrison mutinied and joined the workers in their protest; they set fire to police stations, burst into the jails and released the prisoners.

The Tsar's council of ministers hurriedly turned off the lights and slipped away from their meeting in the Admiralty building. Meanwhile, in the Tauride Palace on the other side of the city, the Duma formed a provisional government, and almost simultaneously, in the same building, the rioting workers and soldiers seized rooms and set up their own political action com-

4

mittee, the Petrograd Soviet. Within days Nicholas abdicated in favor of his brother Mikhail, who in turn relinquished the throne a day later. Thus, after 1,000 years, monarchy in Russia was over. Replacing it was a democracy so divided by factional in-fighting — among intellectuals, small landholders, educated peasants and various shades of radicals in the Petrograd Soviet — that it was little better able to govern than the deposed Romanovs.

Into this situation stepped a man destined to change Russia more profoundly than anyone since Peter the Great. Vladimir Lenin scarcely seemed cast for such a role. Born into the gentry — his father a regional superintendent of schools, his mother a doctor's daughter — he had a perfectly conventional upbringing. Though expelled from university for taking part in a student demonstration, he was never a firebrand until his brother was executed in 1887 for conspiring to assassinate Alexander III. He became a Marxist in 1891, was arrested in 1895, and was sent to Siberia.

On his release in 1900, Lenin left Russia and spent most of the next 17 years abroad, mainly in Switzerland, plotting revolution with the Bolsheviks, one of several radical groups.

When the Romanov regime fell, neither Lenin nor any other Bolshevik participated in the popular uprisings that toppled it. Lenin was still in Switzerland. He got into the fray only with assistance from the German government, which, still at war with Russia, had a natural interest in furthering domestic unrest there.

The Germans agreed to transport Lenin and his party by rail across Germany to Stockholm; no one was to leave the railway carriage or communicate with anyone outside it. (The only person who did violate the pledge was the four-year-old son of one of the Russians, who stuck his head into the neighboring carriage to ask, in French, "What does the conductor do?") They stopped long enough in Stockholm for Lenin to buy a new pair of shoes, on the advice of a companion who said that a man in public life ought to look the part. But when it was suggested that Lenin also buy an overcoat and some extra underwear, he balked, declaring that he was "not going to Petrograd to open a tailor's shop."

From Stockholm, the revolutionaries crossed the Swedish border into Finland on sleighs, then transferred to another train bound for the Russian capital. There, Lenin found a provisional government halfheartedly supported by the workers and soldiers of the Petrograd Soviet but dominated by intellectuals and liberal leaders of the peasantry. His intention was to unseat them by using the Petrograd Soviet as his power base, and he managed to install Bolsheviks in leadership positions in the Soviet. On the eve of November 7, 1917 — October 25 by the old Julian calendar then used in Russia — the Soviet's rank-and-file members, led by Lenin's chief lieutenant, Leon Trotsky, occupied the principal government buildings and arrested the leaders of the provisional government. With this, the October Revolution, the Bolsheviks were in.

They took Russia out of World War I, as the Germans had hoped they would, but another internal war soon started. For the next three years, anti-Communist forces calling themselves the White Army — aided by 14 countries — battled the Red Army (the Communists) for control of the country.

The fighting cost some seven million lives — including those of the Tsar, his wife and his five children.

Although the Tsar had given up his rule over Russia, he had not fled the country, and he and his family were treated gently by the provisional government that initially took over. For five months the imperial family stayed at a summer palace south of Petrograd, but then angry mobs threatened the Romanovs' safety and the provisional government sent them to Siberia — in a manner that was hardly typical of Siberian exile. The family traveled in a private railroad car with a retinue of servants, including seven cooks, 10 footmen, six chambermaids, two valets, a nurse, a doctor, a barber, a butler and a wine steward.

But soon after, the Bolsheviks seized power and the Civil War between the White and Red Armies raged. In April 1918 it was rumored that a White Army detachment might try to free Nicholas. The family was moved to a merchant's house in Ekaterinburg, now called Sverdlovsk, on the eastern slopes of the Ural Mountains. There, at two in the morning on July 18, the prisoners were awakened, taken to the basement and shot with pistols. All were killed by the barrage of bullets except the Tsar's daughter Anastasia, who had to be finished off with bayonets. Their bodies were taken to a nearby mine, where 50 gallons of sulfuric acid and 100 gallons of gasoline were waiting to remove all traces of the execution.

The Civil War dragged on until 1921, but by the end of 1920 the White Army — ill-equipped, outnumbered and lacking in popular support — had been defeated by the Red. By the time the fighting was over, Lenin had consolidated the Communists' power. He died of a stroke in 1924, and two key aides vied to succeed him. One was Leon Trotsky, a Jewish Ukrainian; the other was Josef Stalin, a Georgian whom Lenin had admired for his "expropriations" of funds — bank robberies — to support the Bolsheviks in the days before the Revolution.

The two men differed in their ideologies. Trotsky believed, as had Lenin, that in order for Communism to succeed in Russia, it would have to be part of a worldwide overthrow of capitalism. Stalin, on the other hand, believed that Communism would have to be made to work in Russia before it could be exported.

Stalin had a tremendous political advantage. In 1922, he had been named Secretary General of the Communist Party, and in that position he had filled top government posts with his followers. By December 1927, Trotsky was out and Stalin had taken over. He was to become perhaps the most tyrannical figure in Russian history, heaping on his people repressions that rivaled those of Ivan the Terrible.

Ruthlessly he set out to transform Russia into a world power by increasing its heavy industry with a series of Five-Year Plans. He also organized agriculture into collectives and state farms, overcoming the objections of many peasants with brutal dispossessions and numerous executions.

In the mid-1930s, imagining that opposition to his policies was growing within the leadership, Stalin undertook what has since become known as the Great Purge. Virtually every remaining member of Lenin's original 1917 command group was arrested and tried, then exiled or executed; the same fate was dealt much of the Red Army officer corps, including more than 200 of the top 300 military commanders. In addition, the purge cut a wide swath through the secret-police force, and it liquidated many economists, historians, engineers, scientists, musicians, artists and writers, as well as hundreds of foreign Communists who had the bad luck to be visiting Moscow at the time. The totals are hard to believe: At a conservative estimate, some 20 million people were sent to labor camps; most of them died there.

In all probability Stalin even reached around the world to erase a rival. On August 21, 1940, Leon Trotsky, living in exile in Mexico, was stabbed to death with an alpine pick — almost certainly by Stalin's agents.

The severest test for Stalin's leadership came during World War II. In 1939, Adolph Hitler struck a deal with Stalin, by which they would carve up Poland between them; nevertheless, the Führer later turned on his ally of the moment and marched his troops into the Russian heartland. History was repeating itself, but this time the outcome was different. Instead of buckling under the German juggernaut, the Russians were strong enough to contain and then repel the German forces — thanks in part to Stalin's program of rapid industrialization. The cost in human life was dreadful: at least 20 million Russians killed.

Nevertheless, the Soviet Union emerged from the War the strongest nation in Europe and Asia, a position that Stalin moved quickly to consolidate with a defensive barrier of friendly states under Communist control. This barrier has remained essentially unchanged to the present day.

Stalin's successors continued the relentless drive toward industrialization while simultaneously managing to improve the quality of Soviet life, increasing the supplies of consumer goods and lessening somewhat the repressions of the past. By the 1980s the Union of Soviet Socialist Republics had become a recognized superpower: the world's largest country, rivaling nations of the West in military might, science, industry, culture and global political clout. Thus the dream of Peter the Great was achieved — but only through brutality and totalitarianism. Recalling the cost to the Soviet people, the poet Yevgeni Yevtushenko wrote, "You must remember, when you see the buildings and the dams, what they did to me."

A group of Bolsheviks, in and on an impounded car, stake out an "enemy of the people." During the frenzied weeks following October 25, 1917, such revolutionaries rushed about the Tsarist capital of Petrograd to wipe out opposition.

THE LIVING CHURCH

After more than half a century under an avowedly atheist government, the Russian landscape's most striking man-made features remain the onion domes of its Orthodox churches. More than 7,000 churches are performing rites for crowds of worshippers much as they have over 10 centuries — although before the Revolution, Russia had eight times as many churches to serve half as many people.

Religious activity is actively discouraged by the state. Plainclothes policemen often rough up people attending Easter services; proselytizing is forbidden. Yet the Church not only endures but seems to thrive, tolerated by the government as a useful source of Russian unity, a role it played in World War II. As a result of this uneasy accommodation between state and church, the priesthood attracts educated, serious-minded applicants; congregations have grown, particularly in membership of the young; and the Orthodox Church still glows with some glimmers of the richness of old.

In a traditional ritual, a mitered prelate conducts an Easter procession of monks around Trinity-Saint Sergei monastery in the religious complex of Zagorsk, 44 miles north of Moscow. With six churches and many chapels as well as a seminary, Zagorsk is the spiritual center of Russian Orthodoxy.

An archbishop bearing a staff symbolizing his rank pauses to pet his dog on a walk through his diocese near Moscow. All appointments to church office — from monk to bishop — require government approval.

ASCETICISM IN MONASTERY AND CONVENT

A monk in a monastery near Lvov in the Ukraine observes what the Church calls the discipline of prayer. There are six monasteries in the U.S.S.R., with membership in each limited to about 50. Monks, unlike parish priests, may not marry.

Monks learn manual skills such as welding *(right)* to increase their usefulness to the Church, but monasteries are now purely centers of religious study and no longer engage in commerce or community service.

A nun in her cell in the Convent of the Assumption at Piukhtitsy, Estonia, prays before her order's favored icons. Piukhtitsy is one of 12 active convents, all devoted to ascetic contemplation and worship.

As part of their effort to be self-sufficient, nuns gather wild mushrooms to augment their food supply. They also produce religious accouterments such as bishops' elaborate vestments.

FOR SOME, A REWARDING LIFE

A priest who loves to cook sets a table with traditional Russian dinnerware. Clerics are paid from church donations, and parishioners are generous with gifts.

A bishop receives guests for tea in his residence. His perquisites include a chauffeur-driven limousine and a country cottage.

A parish priest and his family await guests to share their meal amid the plants and flowers of their lace-curtained, chandelier-hung dining room.

Holding candles that symbolize Christ, a couple is married in an Orthodox ceremony after their civil marriage. Such supplementary weddings, rich in tradition, are increasingly popular.

In a church funeral, hymns are sung and prayers read as the dead lie in state. The printed prayers on the chests of the deceased will be placed in their folded hands before burial.

A newly baptized infant is given a symbolic tonsure as other children await their turn. Although baptisms are politically inexpedient — recorded as derogatory notes in parents' dossiers — as many as half the children in some areas are baptized.

On the evening before Easter, a church table is crowded with special cakes, cheeses and eggs brought to be blessed before they are taken home for the festive *razgovenie*, the meal that breaks the Lenten fast. Easter services draw such crowds that admission is often by invitation only — and police outside may harass worshippers as they try to enter.

Despite a January temperature of −4° F., parishioners surround an outdoor altar to celebrate the Epiphany at the 18th Century Church of Saints Constantine and Helen in Suzdal, east of Moscow.

Wearing the peasant costume he often affected, the novelist and nobleman Leo Tolstoy sits among trees on his country estate. This color photograph, taken in 1908 when Tolstoy was 80, is one of a series made for the Tsar by a complex, three-exposure process.

GIANTS OF IMAGINATION

The names themselves, heavy with their cargoes of *k's*, *y's* and *v's*, are at once familiar. When strung together, they suggest the color and richness of the culture their owners helped create: Tolstoy and Dostoyevsky and Chekhov, Pasternak and Solzhenitsyn, Tchaikovsky and Rimsky-Korsakov and Stravinsky, Nijinsky and Pavlova and Diaghilev. And the towering works these great artists have produced — *War and Peace, Crime and Punishment, The Cherry Orchard, The Nutcracker, The Firebird* — also possess a resonance, a strange power that sets them apart from the cultural achievements of other nations.

Like all great works of art, they have a universality that transcends time and place, but there is nonetheless something distinctly Russian about them (although many of their creators were not only ethnic Russians but Ukrainians or Georgians, among others). Their creations evoke a spirit, perhaps, or a tone, or the looming presence of the enormous, abiding land and its people. The physical and spiritual landscape that Leo Tolstoy evoked in *War and Peace* in the 1860s has echoes in Boris Pasternak's 1958 novel *Doctor Zhivago;* it reverberates as well in the symphonies of Peter Tchaikovsky and the ballet music of Igor Stravinsky.

The presence of a distinctive national quality in the work of the best of these artists has certainly contributed both to the vitality of the country's culture and to its tremendous popularity around the world — and at home. Soviet citizens are the world's leading cultural consumers. More books are published,

more movie tickets sold, more theaters and opera houses and dance companies maintained in the Soviet Union than in any other nation. A public reading by a popular poet or the debut of a new ballet generates the rambunctious excitement that Western Europeans and Americans associate with championship athletic competitions or rock concerts. The publication of a new book by a major author creates long lines outside bookstores — which are swiftly followed by a black market in hoarded copies when the edition runs out.

But perhaps the most remarkable aspect of this culture is its achievement of such greatness and popularity in an environment hostile to individual creativity. During most of the last century and a half — the comparatively brief span in which virtually all of the great works were produced — all forms of art have been subject to the dictatorial control of oppressive governments. In the 19th Century the autocratic Romanov Tsars tried to stifle any criticism of their regimes. Since the late 1920s the Soviet rulers have not only refused to allow criticism, but have also demanded that painters, writers and even musicians create works praising the state and its ideology. Stalin declared that artistic freedom was a bourgeois delusion; the purpose of art was to exalt the regime. Since Stalin's death in 1953, his successors in the Kremlin have tolerated sporadic bursts of creative independence, but these brief thaws have invariably been followed by new freezes. All artists in the Soviet Union must live and work under Big Brother's unblinking gaze.

Censorship under the Tsars was not as fierce or as efficient as it has been under the Soviet government. The tsarist watchdogs, according to this century's brilliant Russian-born (but self-exiled) novelist Vladimir Nabokov, were mostly "muddled old reactionaries that clustered around the shivering throne." They often had trouble spotting subversion if it was cloaked under even a thin disguise — and the artists quickly became adept in Aesopian language, that is, in disguising what they wished to say as fables and tall tales.

Russia's 19th Century artists also escaped some modern strictures: They might be forbidden to criticize the tsarist regimes, but they were not forced to praise them. Many of Russia's pioneering writers, composers and painters were "quite certain that they lived in a country of oppression and slavery," noted Nabokov, but they had "the immense advantage over their grandsons in modern Russia of not being compelled to say that there was no oppression and no slavery."

The artists of tsarist times had sufficient freedom to convey an astonishing amount of truth, and they did so first in literature, which exploded into new life in the early years of the 19th Century. Western ideas and books, which had been flooding into the country since the 17th Century reign of Tsar Peter the Great, had caused tremendous intellectual ferment. Reacting to these ideas, writers began creating numbers of powerful works. Perhaps no other nation, in a single century, has produced more great novels, poems and plays.

5

Alexander Pushkin won undying fame for his poetry — and notoriety for his card playing. The police kept a dossier on him that was headed, "No. 36, Pushkin, well-known gambler."

The man who ignited the explosion was Alexander Pushkin, recognized as the nation's greatest poet. Born in Moscow in 1799, he grew up to be small, wiry, precociously clever and, with his exotically dusky complexion — inherited from his great-grandfather, an Ethiopian prince named Ibrahim Hannibal, who had been adopted by the great Peter himself — irresistible to women.

Pushkin published his first verse at the age of 15 and was famous before he was 20, both for his poetry and for his pursuit of titled women, ballerinas and prostitutes. He soon began keeping a list of his conquests, dividing them into two categories, "Platonic" and "Sexual." His wicked wit and magnetism made him the darling of St. Petersburg's drawing rooms, much like the fashionable young man he portrays in his great novel in verse, *Eugene Onegin:*

His hair cut in the latest mode,
He dined, he danced, he fenced, he rode.
In French he could converse politely,
As well as write; and how he bowed!
In the mazurka, 'twas allowed,
No partner ever was so sprightly.
What more is asked? The world is warm
In praise of so much wit and charm.

The world was warm, but the officials around Tsar Alexander I were anything but charmed by the young poet's behavior: His womanizing involved him in duels and he gambled and drank to excess. Nor were they enamored of his clever epigrams mocking church and state, or of the audacious *Ode to Liberty* that he wrote in Russian — in a magically pellucid, elegant way. He was hustled into exile in faraway Kishinev, a forlorn outpost in southern Russia.

But exile did not quiet Pushkin. He wrote more clever and subversive poems, gambled and drank with the Ki-

shinev Army garrison, and romanced the local women. He also took part in more duels. He arrived at one such dawn appointment — with a man whom he had accused of cheating at cards — nonchalantly munching some cherries. He popped one into his mouth just before the signal to fire was given. His adversary fired and missed. Pushkin, who had not deigned to shoot, dropped his pistol, spat the cherry pit in his enemy's direction and coolly strolled off.

The Tsar's officials eventually transferred their problem poet to Odessa to work in a government office, but then banished him to his family's estate near Pskov, west of Leningrad. There, Pushkin read voraciously, absorbed Russian folk tales told by his boyhood nurse and wrote prodigiously. So great is the power of Pushkin's best tales and poems that more than 20 operas — including the popular *Boris Godunov* — have been based on his works.

With the accession of a new Tsar, Nicholas I, in 1825, Pushkin was summoned back to the capital, where he became the Tsar's private, and captive, poet. The starchy and militaristic Tsar appointed him to various court positions but also insisted on personally overseeing his writing. The secret police kept tabs on the poet's after-hours escapades. Pushkin continued to produce fine poetry and prose despite his imperial censor, and he also resumed his rousing lifestyle, although his philandering was tempered by marriage in 1831 to a beautiful if vacuous 18-year-old (according to Pushkin, this was the 113th time he had fallen in love).

His bride, Natalya, was a dazzling addition to the court, and before long the Tsar himself was discreetly flirting with her while his tethered poet quietly fumed. Pushkin was further humiliat-

ed when the Tsar made him a gentleman of the chamber, a post he could not refuse, primarily to ensure his wife's presence at court. Soon Natalya and a glamorous French baron named Georges-Charles D'Anthès began to spend an eyebrow-raising amount of time together. Pushkin continued to fume but did nothing until he received anonymous letters mocking him as a cuckold. Suspicion has since arisen that government officials, perceiving a stratagem that might rid them of the obstreperous poet, arranged for the letters to be sent. This insult spurred Pushkin to challenge D'Anthès. The French baron's bullet struck Pushkin in the upper thigh and penetrated deep into the abdomen. After two days of agony Pushkin died, aged 37, while by his bed his wife blubbered, "Forgive me!"

His death prompted an outpouring of public grief; more than 30,000 people filed by his casket in a single day. Notables and newspapers eulogized the poet, but the most moving tribute was offered by an elderly citizen who was seen weeping bitterly by the coffin. Asked if he had known Pushkin, the old man replied, "No, but I am a Russian."

Pushkin set the stage for the great writers that would follow, especially in one of his last works, a long, brooding poem called *The Bronze Horseman*. His themes — the conflict between the individual and the state, the powerlessness of frail humans in the face of the forces of nature, the dangerous irrational depths within all human beings — preoccupied his two immediate successors, the poet Mikhail Lermontov and the playwright and novelist Nikolai Gogol. Lermontov — who died even younger than Pushkin, shot dead in a duel at the age of 26 in 1841 — wrote outspoken political verses attacking the hypocrisy and stupidity of the ruling class. He produced subjective poems that prefigure the psychological probings of later writers. In *The Demon* he imagines a malign figure who proclaims:

I am he, whose gaze destroys hope,
As soon as hope blooms;
I am he, whom nobody loves,
And everything that lives curses.

And he dwelled on the Russians' ambivalent but stubborn love for their land. In a brief poem, "My Country," Lermontov opens by proclaiming that "I love my country, but that love is odd: / My reason has no part in it at all!" and then continues:

Ask me not why I love, but love I must
Her fields' cold silences,
Her somber forests swaying in a gust,
Her rivers at the flood like seas.

Gogol loved his country equally, or said he did. He was a political conservative and a defender of tsarist autocracy. But when he sat down to write, his fantastic imagination created a nightmare land, a sprawling, ugly, ramshackle country peopled by grotesques. His satiric play *The Inspector General* presents a

One of the magnificent Easter eggs made by Russia's greatest jeweler, Carl Fabergé, holds a dozen tiny views of royal residences in a quartz globe adorned with diamonds, enamel and gold. Starting in 1884, the French-descended Fabergé did more than 50 of these *objets d'art* — masterpieces of imagination and craftsmanship — for the imperial family. This one was a gift from Nicholas II to his wife in 1896.

hilariously inept group of petty officials in a provincial town. The mayor, Gogol says, is "a grafter" adept at quick switches from "servility to arrogance"; the judge, who also takes bribes, "wheezes and huffs like an antique clock that hisses before it strikes the hour"; the postmaster opens everybody's mail; the Director of Charities scandalously neglects the patients in his hospital — "stick some clean gowns on the patients," the mayor tells him. "I don't want them looking like a gang of chimney sweeps" — and the teachers and policemen are lunatics or drunks, or both.

But *The Inspector General* is outdone by Gogol's great (and only) novel, *Dead Souls* (finished in 1842), which offers an unmatched rogues' gallery of bizarre creatures. The plot is itself a mordant Gogolian joke. A swindler named Chichikov travels the countryside, buying dead serfs (or "souls") from provincial landlords and, armed with the papers proving his ownership of these deceased workers, sells them to unsuspecting buyers as if they were alive. In the course of his dealings, Chichikov encounters what seems to be the entire rural population — landlords, innkeepers, serfs, coachmen, petty officials. Every one of them is misshapen, physically and spiritually, in some strange way.

Among the writers whose genius dominated the latter half of the century — Turgenev, Tolstoy and Dostoyevsky — it was Feodor Dostoyevsky who most revered Gogol. His work also gives somber pictures of the country, lit by episodes of fantastic comedy. The shy, epileptic son of a not-very-successful and evidently foul-tempered physician, Dostoyevsky received the first of the shocks that marred his life when his father was killed by some of his serfs. Whether or not the young Dostoyevsky

had wished, consciously or subconsciously, for his abusive father's death, patricide became a dominant theme in his novel *The Brothers Karamazov,* and he was always fascinated by violent crime and the criminal mentality.

His family was impoverished by the father's death, and Dostoyevsky felt himself among the downtrodden. His sympathy for society's victims led him to join a group of young radicals that was ferreted out in short order by the tsarist police. Dostoyevsky and 20 others were tried and sentenced to death. Three days before Christmas in 1849, the conspirators were dressed in white shrouds and brought before a firing squad, but at the last minute the execution was halted on orders from the Tsar; one man was led away insane. Dostoyevsky was banished to Siberia for four years of hard labor and several years of Army service. Eventually pardoned by Tsar Alexander II, he chronicled his prison experiences in *House of the Dead,* the first of the scarifying accounts of life in Russian prison camps that ever since have continued to appear — as in Alexander Solzhenitsyn's *One Day in the Life of Ivan Denisovitch.*

These experiences did not turn Dostoyevsky into a confirmed revolutionary. Rather, they converted him to Slavophilism, a belief that only in Russia and her Slavic peoples, and in the Christianity of the Orthodox Church, was there salvation from the corrupting influence of Western materialist ideas.

Dostoyevsky's views coalesced in the first great novel he wrote after his return from Siberia, *Crime and Punishment.* The hero — who is also the villain — is an impoverished young student named Raskolnikov. He commits a hideous crime, splitting the skulls of an elderly woman moneylender and her sister with a hatchet. Robbery is one motive, but another is drawn from Raskolnikov's reading of German philosophers who seemed to preach that a "superior" man had the right to crush lesser humans on his path to greatness.

Raskolnikov has hardly committed the murders, however, before being overwhelmed by feelings of guilt. He is "seized with panic," Dostoyevsky writes, "not because of any fear for himself, but in sheer horror and disgust at what he had done." Back in his own room, he falls into a stupor, awakening only to recall the grisly murder scene and to be assailed by "the conviction that everything, even his memory, even plain common sense, was abandoning him. . . . 'What if,' Raskolnikov thinks in his near-delirium, 'it is already beginning, if my punishment is already beginning? Yes, yes, that is so!'"

Remorse drives Raskolnikov to commit one subconscious blunder after another, to follow a path of irrational behavior that inevitably reveals his guilt to the police. Tried, convicted and sent to Siberia, he achieves salvation — explains Dostoyevsky in an almost apocalyptic ending — through suffering, humility, the Bible and a new-found ability to love his fellows. "Life had taken the place of dialectics," Dostoyevsky writes, heralding "the gradual rebirth of a man," his "gradual passing from one world to another."

Dostoyevsky wrote *Crime and Punishment* in little more than a year. Like his hero, he was tormented by debt. A literary magazine he had been running collapsed. Then his brother died, leaving Dostoyevsky to provide for the widow and children. Worst of all, he was a compulsive gambler, often losing at roulette every ruble he possessed.

But slowly, with enormous effort, he

VENERATED RELICS OF MUSCOVITE ART

This 12th Century icon of Christ, done in Novgorod, shows the Byzantine influence.

Among the greatest treasures of Russia are the thousands of icons — religious paintings on wood panels — that were produced by anonymous artists in monasteries and church-sponsored workshops from the 11th Century through the 17th. These paintings not only portrayed Christ, the Virgin, saints and angels, but were also holy objects themselves, to be prayed to and venerated. Icons hung in every church and household; many were credited with miraculous powers to cure the sick or repel foreign invaders.

Because icons were holy, they were not meant to be realistic. They were two-dimensional, lacking the illusion of depth that Renaissance artists in the West were pursuing at that time. Nor did icon painters strive for originality. Rather, icons were patterned after time-honored designs laid down in a handbook, the *Podlinnik*.

The artists were free, however, to experiment with color. Their brilliant hues, combined with strong and simple designs, make the finest of these holy images powerful works of art as well as eloquent testimony to the deep Christian faith of Old Russia.

wrote his way out of debt. *Crime and Punishment* was a success, and he followed it with a novel about a simple-minded Christian saint, called *The Idiot.* This was followed by the works some critics consider his masterpieces, *The Possessed* and *The Brothers Karamazov.*

The title of *The Possessed* is sometimes translated as *The Devils.* The devils in question are a group of would-be revolutionaries whose goal is a materialist Russia free of all moral restraints. In a devastating vision of this new political state and its amoral freedom, Dostoyevsky prefigures remarkably the totalitarian regimes of the 20th Century. "I'm afraid I got rather muddled up in my own data," one revolutionary says, "and my conclusion is in direct contradiction to the original idea with which I started. Starting from unlimited freedom, I arrived at unlimited despotism."

Another describes this despotism:

"Every member of the society spies on the others, and he is obliged to inform against them. Everyone belongs to all the others, and all belong to everyone. All are slaves and equals in slavery." Creative genius, disruptive of totalitarian order, was to be eradicated: "A Cicero will have his tongue cut out, Copernicus will have his eyes gouged out, a Shakespeare will be stoned." The only thing the new state will want, he adds, "is obedience. The only thing that's wanting in the world is obedience."

One character in the book, Shatov, seems to speak for Dostoyevsky. "I believe in Russia," he says. "I believe in the Orthodox Church. I — I believe in the body of Christ — I believe that the Second Coming will take place in Russia."

After immersion in Dostoyevsky's dark and tormented world, it is like emerging into the sunlight to read the works of Tolstoy. Not that violence and

Fancifully decorated window frames
like these adorn many of Siberia's
wooden houses. This traditional folk
art includes intricate fretwork
often enlivened by stylized birds and
flowers *(opposite, center)*.

anguish have no place in his novels. In *War and Peace* he describes Napoleon's 1812 invasion of Russia in gory detail; his other long novel, *Anna Karenina*, ends with the heroine, Anna, throwing herself in despair under a train. His characters are mostly quite sane, and his heroes are eminently so; they play out their dramas for the most part in daylight and in the open countryside. In contrast to Dostoyevsky's fevered writing, Tolstoy's prose is clear, leisurely and as naturally paced as a heartbeat.

In origin the two writers were as different as their works, yet they arrived at very similar conclusions about humanity's need for spiritual regeneration through the teachings of Christ. Tolstoy was born in 1828 to aristocratic ease and privilege, heir of a count, on his family's 4,000-acre estate at Yasnaya Polyana, 130 miles south of Moscow.

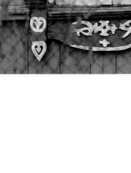

Singularly gifted and energetic, he forged a career that brimmed with contradictions: He was an officer's son and an officer himself, who chronicled war but later embraced pacifism, a nobleman who habitually wore peasant garb, a sophisticate who preferred the bucolic life of the countryside, a great writer who eventually renounced literature. In his youth he gambled and caroused in St. Petersburg but then, disgusted with his profligacy, he fled the city for the Caucasus Mountains. Shortly afterward, Tolstoy served in the Crimean War, and his published account of the siege of Sevastopol helped establish his reputation as a promising author.

Literature then, as later, did not command Tolstoy's entire attention. He returned to Yasnaya Polyana and, always concerned for the welfare of the workers on the family estate, started a special school for the peasant children, and

5

himself served as the principal teacher. He also did heavy labor in the fields.

Tolstoy added to this taxing regime the writing of *War and Peace*. The novel, published between 1865 and 1869 in six volumes, is most remarkable perhaps for its inclusiveness. All human life seems to be here, from what one character, Prince Andrei, calls the "best human attributes — love, poetry, tenderness," to the brutalities of war on a vast scale. Birth, marriage and familial love are included, along with unfulfilled hopes, heartbreak and death. Tolstoy took pains to give each of his many characters a distinctive personality and voice; one critic noted that even the book's dogs are individualized. Tolstoy's characterizations are deft. Introducing an elderly aristocrat who is a master of vacuous chitchat, Tolstoy has him utter an insincere compliment and then adds, "like a wound-up clock, by force of habit [he] said things he did not even wish to be believed."

Even the completion of this huge masterpiece left Tolstoy feeling unfulfilled. He resumed teaching, brooded about religion and hurled himself into the simple satisfactions of physical labor. "I work, chop, spade, mow and do not give one thought to literature and those awful literary folk," he wrote a friend. But soon he was working on the lengthy portrayal of the Russian upper crust that became *Anna Karenina*. Dostoyevsky, a friend reported, was so excited by the book that he ran around St. Petersburg, "waving his hands and calling Tolstoy the god of art." But the god of art himself soon soured on his own creation; his religious ruminations had convinced him that all art was ungodly because it was based on imagination — that is to say, deceit — and he called even his own *Anna* "an abomi-nation that no longer exists for me."

In his last three decades Tolstoy embarked on a search for a mystical inner truth — *istina*, in Russian — rather in the manner of one of Dostoyevsky's redeemed sinners. He became something of a holy man to whom others made pilgrimages and, protected from official persecution by his worldwide fame, he became a savage critic both of the government and of the Orthodox Church. He swore off meat, wine, hunting and smoking, advocated nonviolent resistance to authority and developed his own quirky brand of Christianity. He was still following his own quixotic impulses when he died of pneumonia in 1910 at the age of 82. He had fled from a discordant marriage to join a band of his religious followers in the Caucasus, where he was stricken at a village railroad station. His last words were fittingly Tolstoyan: "The truth . . . I love man . . . How are they . . ."

Like Pushkin and Tolstoy, their celebrated contemporary Ivan Turgenev was born to wealth: His family at one time owned as many as 5,000 serfs, including a company of musicians that formed an all-serf orchestra; the sole duty of other serfs was to feed the Turgenev pigeons. As a young novelist he assailed the institution of serfdom and had the satisfaction of contributing to its abolition in 1861, but he paid the price for protest — a brief jail term and two years' house arrest.

Turgenev was an ardent admirer of Western culture — especially the technical virtuosity of the French novelist Gustave Flaubert — and his works lack the intensity found in the novels of Tolstoy and Dostoyevsky. But few writers ever more gracefully described the Russian countryside. In *Fathers and Sons*, he offers a vision of a country eve-

The implacable hostility of Stalin and his successors to all modern art has obscured the fact that for a brief, heady period between 1910 and 1930, Russian painters and sculptors were by far the most daring of the avant-garde. A few of these inventive artists — notably Vasily Kandinsky and Marc Chagall — fled Soviet orthodoxy to win fame in the West, but they were only part of an astonishingly productive group, now almost forgotten, who pioneered modern art.

Many of the Russians studied in Paris and other hotbeds of experimental art before World War I and brought home the inspiration of Picasso, Matisse and others. But they then carried experimental forms to new extremes, with innovations that only later appeared in the West. Under the banners of several "isms" — Rayonism, Constructivism, Suprematism — such painters as Kazimir Malevich and Mikhail Matiushin (*top right*) did away with all realistic elements and created pure abstractions — geometric arrangements of line and color — with such titles as "Red Square in Black" and "Counter Relief."

For a brief period after the political revolution of 1917 this revolutionary art won government approval, and a number of the artists, among them El Lissitzky (*right*), devoted their talents to the new Soviet state. But the Kremlin gradually turned against their abstract modes, and in the early 1930s Stalin completed the destruction of the avant-garde by decreeing that all art must be "comprehensible to the millions"; the only permissible mode became a mawkish representational style, "Socialist Realism" (*far right*).

RISE AND FALL OF A PRECOCIOUS, DARING AVANT-GARDE

Bands of luminous colors flash across an abstract painting entitled "Movement in Space," done in 1918 by the musician and artist Mikhail Matiushin. It prefigured by 40 years the work of the schools of Abstract Expressionist painting after World War II. Matiushin's music was equally unconventional; one composition included cannon shots and the sounds of a crashing airplane.

A 1919 political poster of geometric forms by El Lissitzky, "Beat the Whites with the Red Wedge," exhorts the Communist Red Army to defeat its Civil War enemy, the White forces.

In sharp contrast to the fresh work of the avant-garde is this trite Socialist Realist painting by Efim Cheptsov, in which a uniformed party worker addresses villagers in a local theater.

5

ning: "The sun had hid behind a small aspen grove" that spread its shadow "across the still fields. A peasant could be seen riding at a trot on a white horse along a dark narrow path skirting that distant grove" as the "setting sun flushed the trunks of the aspen-trees with such a warm glow that they seemed the color of pine-trunks."

The last of the great 19th Century writers, Anton Chekhov, was the grandson of a serf, born in 1860 to a poor family in the provincial city of Taganrog. He worked his way through school, then supported himself and his family by scribbling comic sketches for newspapers and magazines while studying medicine in Moscow.

But these difficult years did not embitter Chekhov. He became the most cheerful and sociable of men—ready always, noted a friend, "to sing with the singers and to get drunk with the drunkards." Devotedly public-spirited, he worked long hours as a physician in Moscow's poor suburbs, mostly without pay; during a cholera epidemic he alone cared for the sick in 25 villages; he built four schools for peasant children entirely with his own funds; he made an exhausting trip to a tsarist prison colony on the Pacific island of Sakhalin and wrote an account of life there, simply because he felt it his civic duty to investigate prison conditions. Even after he contracted the tuberculosis that would kill him at the age of 44, he was not deflected from his concern for people around him. In a letter to a friend he wrote, "If every man did what he could on his little bit of soil, how marvelous our world would be!"

Despite all his activities, he managed to create what a critic called "that colossal, encyclopedically detailed Russian world of the 1880s and 1890s which goes by the name of *Chekhov's Short Stories*." These narratives advance no political theories but portray in plain language the lives of the people: peasants and intellectuals, aristocrats and clerks, landowners and the hopelessly poor. The stories are sometimes humorous, but the humor is always mixed with sadness. In one, "In the Ravine," an aged peasant comforts a poor woman whose baby has died: " 'Never mind,' he repeated. 'Yours is not the worst of sorrows. Life is long, there is good and bad yet to come, there is everything to come. Great is Mother Russia.' "

This melancholy also suffuses Chekhov's plays, which portray idealistic intellectuals unable to translate their ideals into action. In *The Three Sisters*, a trio of sensitive provincial women resolve to go to Moscow—to achieve something, perhaps, or at least to see some of life—but they never leave their crumbling country estate. In *Uncle Vanya*, a frustrated idealist, desperate at his own ineffectuality, tries twice to shoot the man he believes responsible for his wasted life—and misses. In *The Cherry Orchard,* an impoverished family is powerless to prevent the forced sale of part of their property; the last sound in the play is of axes chopping down their beloved orchard. Sonya, the heroine of *Uncle Vanya*, speaks for all Chekhov characters: "There is nothing for it. We shall live through a long chain of days and weary evenings; we shall patiently bear the trials which fate sends us." And she adds: "When our time comes we shall die without a murmur."

The richness of the golden age of Russian literature was equaled in the performing arts of the 19th and early 20th Centuries. In music and dance especially, creative geniuses in Russia set world standards. And like the writers of their time, they imbued their works with quintessentially Russian intensity.

During the years when Tolstoy, Dostoyevsky and Turgenev were writing, Peter Tchaikovsky was composing his brooding, romantic symphonies, and a group of gifted amateurs known as the "Mighty Handful" were joining him in lifting Russian music to a new eminence. The composers, like the writers, drew heavily on peasant folklore, and they filled their scores with the same spaciousness and gentle rhythms that Turgenev and other writers employed to evoke the land. The musical outpouring included symphonies and operas as well as compositions that helped make Russian ballet preeminent.

The most prominent members of the Mighty Handful were Alexander Borodin, Modest Mussorgsky and Nikolai Rimsky-Korsakov, bound together not only by friendship, but also by a common lack of classical musical training and the fact that all of them had other, nonmusical careers: Borodin was a professor of chemistry, Mussorgsky a government official and Rimsky-Korsakov a naval officer. For a time Mussorgsky and Rimsky-Korsakov shared a St. Petersburg apartment furnished with a piano and a single table. Mussorgsky used the piano in the morning while Rimsky-Korsakov wrote at the table; in the afternoon Rimsky-Korsakov took over the piano while Mussorgsky worked in a government office.

Borodin, the illegitimate son of a Georgian prince, taught himself to play the violin and cello and composed his first concerto when he was 13. After earning his chemistry degree and studying in Western Europe for four years, he returned to St. Petersburg and began composing in his spare time. He eventually produced two symphonies and the unfinished opera *Prince Igor,* which Rimsky-Korsakov completed after Borodin died in 1887. The opera's "Polovtsian Dances" segment, redolent of Russia's Asiatic East, is perhaps his best-known legacy.

Mussorgsky, musically the most radical member of the group, tried to reproduce the sounds of nature and even Russian speech in his often nonmelodic compositions. *Night on Bald Mountain,* written in 11 days, was an explosive depiction of a Ukrainian witches'-Sabbath ceremony. The 1874 production of his masterly opera *Boris Godunov* was both the culmination of his career and the beginning of his sad, alcoholic decline. He was devastated when the opera was dropped after only 20 performances and — cursed by an unstable and self-destructive personality — he had drunk himself to death by the age of 42.

Rimsky-Korsakov was the youngest and most prolific of the three. Son of a provincial governor, he became a naval officer and spent three years sailing the world with the Imperial Fleet. His musical talent was recognized by the court and he was given a professorship at the St. Petersburg conservatory, followed by a special assignment as inspector of naval bands. These appointments freed him to compose. In 15 operas and numerous symphonic pieces, such as the popular *Scheherazade* suite, Rimsky-Korsakov drew his inspiration and melodies directly from Russian folk music; he once trailed a servant around a friend's house "to catch a tricky rhythm" in a tune she was singing. In later years he was world-famous as both a composer and conductor, becoming director of the Imperial Russian Symphony and the lone foreign member of the French Academy.

Looming above these three was the

A muscular young ballet student practices classic movements in one of Moscow's many dance schools. So great is the Russian passion for ballet that there are 40 major dance companies flourishing in the nation.

unique and majestic figure of Peter Ilyich Tchaikovsky, the greatest composer of the golden age. Trained as a lawyer, he turned to music in his twenties, persisting in spite of critical disparagement so severe that he burned some of his scores in despair. Gaining prominence with his symphony *Winter Dreams* in 1868, he went on to produce a magnificent repertoire of symphonies, operas such as *Eugene Onegin,* and the classic ballets *Swan Lake, The Nutcracker* and *Sleeping Beauty.* Ballet had been popular in Russia for many years — Pushkin called it "soul-inspired flight" — but Tchaikovsky's collaboration with the French-born Marius Petipa, director of the imperial ballet, culminated Petipa's long campaign to elevate Russian dance to international supremacy.

Tchaikovsky rejected the nationalism of the Mighty Handful; his aim was to compose music that "explored the human soul." His explanation of his choice of Shakespeare's *Romeo and Juliet* as the subject of an opera is characteristic: "There are no Tsars," he said, "no marches, there is nothing that consti-

tutes the routine of an opera. There is only love, love and love." The music in his six symphonies, alternately joyful and intensely melancholy, joins a distinctive Russian sensibility to a humanity that transcends political borders.

By the time Tchaikovsky died, in 1893, Russian literature, music and dance were universally recognized as world treasures. In the ensuing three decades of political ferment, Russians would lead the way in new art forms such as film and abstract painting, while a new generation of writers and composers revitalized literature and music with exciting experimentation.

The era that began in the 1890s and ended with Stalin's crackdown in the early 1930s was a time of growth. By the eve of the Revolution, there were 6,000 newspapers and magazines published in Moscow and St. Petersburg alone. A hundred poets earned their living with their pens. The theatrical genius Konstantin Stanislavsky introduced a new and much-emulated acting technique — "the Method" — at his innovative Moscow Art Theater. The Russian ballet, with Stravinsky's music and inspired choreography by Sergei Diaghilev, became clearly the best in the world, exporting spectacular productions starring such virtuoso dancers as Anna Pavlova and Vaclav Nijinsky. (Nijinsky's leaps were so prodigious that skeptics checked his shoes for rubber and the stage for mechanical aids; the dancer explained disingenuously that the trick was "to go up and then pause a little up there.")

The heavy hand of Stalinist conformity brought an end to this effervescent time. Since then the government has strictly monitored all the arts, chiefly through the various national unions to which writers, composers and other

5

artists must belong. Established when Stalin was consolidating his power in the early 1930s, the unions spelled out the artist's role as political cheerleader. The Union of Soviet Writers defined its goal as "the creation of works" that would be "saturated with the heroic struggles of the world proletariat" and would "reflect the great wisdom and heroism of the Communist Party." Similar standards were enunciated by the unions of musicians and painters. The works that adhered to these prescriptions — novels extolling construction projects, heroic portraits of party leaders — have won little recognition outside the U.S.S.R.

The Writers' Union has enforced its policies through its ownership of book-publishing houses and literary magazines and has prevented the appearance of any material diverging from the party line. The union can even keep nonmembers from earning their living. Joseph Brodsky, a dissident poet who did not belong to the union, was prosecuted for continuing to write poetry. A judge ordered him to produce "documentary evidence" proving he had the right to compose verse, then ruled that he was a "parasite." Eventually Brodsky served 18 months of hard labor. He was forced to emigrate in 1972.

Despite such persecution and omnipresent censorship, some 20th Century writers have managed to say what they wanted to, and have produced works that rival those of their great predecessors. The popular poets, who draw thousands to their public readings, are generally circumspect onstage, but they too provide a tangy note of nonconformity now and again. The best known in the West, Yevgeny Yevtushenko, has drifted out of official favor as his verses nudged the limits of governmental tolerance.

Other writers, such as the acclaimed poet Anna Akhmatova, have taken greater risks and have often suffered for it. Akhmatova's first husband was killed, and her third husband and her son were imprisoned in labor camps. She was barred from publishing her work and expelled from the union. Still, in lines that were eventually heard, she expressed the anguish of the artist in chains:

For some the wind can freshly blow,
For some the sunlight fade at ease,
But we, made partners in our dread,
Hear but the grating of the keys,
And heavy-booted soldiers' tread.

Another of the more courageous was Boris Pasternak, whose refusal to praise the party in conventional verse made his life a perilous transit of the minefields of Soviet officialdom. For most of his career Pasternak was a lyric poet with a gift for evoking nature and an intensely personal style. By 1934 he had attained such stature that Stalin telephoned one day to ask his opinion of the works of the dissident poet Osip Mandelstam. Pasternak praised Mandelstam highly and tried to change the subject. He wanted to have a long talk with the supreme leader, he said later, "about love, about life, about death," but Stalin cut the conversation short.

Two years afterward Pasternak "confessed" at a writers' congress that his temperament was incompatible with "socialist realism." Censured as a result, he was prevented from publishing his work for the next seven years. He probably would have suffered worse punishment had not a friend been head of the Writers' Union.

In the mid-1940s Pasternak began a novel, *Doctor Zhivago*. "In it I want to convey the historical image of Russia over the past 45 years," he wrote. "It is literature in a deeper sense than anything I have ever done." When he finally finished the book, he was not allowed to publish it. He smuggled the manuscript to Italy, and the novel appeared to international acclaim in 1957.

Doctor Zhivago won Pasternak a Nobel Prize, but the government forced him to decline it and he was reviled as a counterrevolutionary demon. The two years that remained before he died at 70 in 1960 were clouded by harass-

Muscovites throng an outdoor exhibit of paintings — conventional by Western standards but avant-garde in the U.S.S.R. This show was put on with official permission; an earlier one was crushed by police bulldozers.

ment and forced isolation. Nevertheless, his admirers make an annual pilgrimage to his grave on the anniversary of his death.

Other writers who have produced works that they know the censors will reject have resorted to a clandestine form of publishing — typed manuscripts that are passed around by a select circle of readers. This process of *samizdat* (self-publishing) often obliges the recipient of a manuscript to keep the ball rolling by making additional copies; hundreds of underground copies of Alexander Solzhenitsyn's damning study of the penal system, *The Gulag Archipelago,* were reportedly produced in this way. *Magnitizdat,* the private recording and circulation of im-

politic songs on tape cassettes, is an electronic version of *samizdat.*

Another method of circumventing the watchdogs is the use of the old technique of Aesopian language — slipping a heretical notion about modern Russia into a tale set in a distant time or place, even another planet. A science-fiction novel called *It's Difficult to Be God,* by the brothers Boris and Arkady Strugatsky, depicts a despotic — and familiar — society created by space travelers who settle on another planet. A recent restaging of *Hamlet* presented the melancholy Dane as an angry firebrand battling against an evil tyrant — while theatergoers smiled in recognition.

A few obstinate artists have forgone such subterfuges for open, perhaps

foolhardy, defiance of censorship with savage attacks on the Soviet establishment. One of the most bravely recalcitrant was the poet Mandelstam. He tangled repeatedly with the Kremlin, suffering more severe reprisals each time. He sealed his fate by writing a bitter poetic assault on Stalin, whom he described as "the Kremlin mountaineer, the murderer" with a "cockroach whiskers leer" and "fingers fat as grubs." For this "counterrevolutionary activity" Mandelstam was sent to a prison camp in 1937, where he died of unexplained causes within a year. It was Mandelstam who once had said, "Russia is the only place where poetry is really important — they'll kill people for it here."

Poet Bella Akhmadulina poses for husband Boris Messerer in his Moscow studio. A fellow poet once called her "a fatal show-off," an "angel from another

A BLESSED COUPLE

Bella and Boris Messerer are among the Soviet elite, distinguished citizens rewarded for their achievements with a life style that would be considered comfortable in any society. Boris is an artist and set designer. Bella—known to her millions of fans by her maiden name, Akhmadulina—is a translator and one of the country's most famous poets, who often gives large, well-attended public readings. Her poetry is lyrical, deeply feminine and apolitical *(below)*.

While more ordinary citizens may be living in cramped quarters, the Messerer family—Bella and Boris, Bella's two young daughters from her previous marriages and their pet poodle and German shepherd—enjoy well-furnished homes in city and country. They have a three-room dacha, or country cottage, in the village of Peredelkino just 20 miles from Moscow. Here, nestled among the trees, are other wooden dachas of writers and editors. The houses were built by the Writers' Union for its most illustrious members; they may be owned outright or rented for a nominal fee. In addition to their Peredelkino dacha, the Messerers have a handsome apartment with studio *(right)* in an old Moscow building, where Boris paints in bold, contemporary style.

DON'T GIVE ME ALL OF YOUR TIME

Don't give me all of your time,
don't question me so often.
With eyes so true and faithful
don't try and catch my hands.

Don't follow in the Spring
my steps through pools of rain.
I know that of our meeting
nothing will come again.

You think it's pride that makes
me turn my back on you?
It's grief, not pride that holds
my head so very straight.

Bella Akhmadulina, 1962

Standing tall in spike heels, Bella recites her poems in an elaborately decorated Moscow concert hall. In the Soviet Union, such readings are second in popularity only to soccer; the poet Andrei Voznesensky once filled an ice-hockey stadium with more than 10,000 of his admirers.

Bella is interviewed by a Moscow television crew. Her face is well-known throughout the country, not only because of her poetry, but because of her frequent television appearances. She also once starred in a hit movie, playing the part of a brash reporter.

Boris, who divides his time between his painting and set designs for theater, opera and ballet productions, adjusts the model of a modern stage set he is working on. Boris is also an accomplished printmaker and keeps a large hand press in his studio.

After writing poetry all morning long, Bella begins preparations for lunch in her modern, well-equipped Moscow kitchen. Hanging on the wall are dough sculptures.

The couple lunches in their sunken dining/sitting room, an unusual architectural feature of their prerevolutionary top-floor apartment. The old-fashioned phonograph in the foreground is one of several belonging to Boris, who collects antiques.

Boris shows off one of the century-old samovars he collects and displays on a 19th Century sideboard.

At day's end Bella and Boris relax in front of a fire while she reads him some of her fan mail. Fireplaces are rare in Moscow, where most housing is built from prefabricated sections.

A QUIET PLACE IN THE COUNTRY

Boris wears modish ski clothes — including a wool cap from Lake Placid, New York, scene of the 1980 Winter Olympics — as he wields a Russian wooden shovel to clear snow from the steps of the couple's country house.

Entertaining a guest in their pine-paneled dacha, Bella lays a table with a variety of cold appetizers — as well as imported Danish beer with which to wash down the food. At far left is Bella's younger daughter, Lisa.

In homage to famed writer Boris Pasternak, Bella leaves flowers on his grave at Peredelkino, a shrine to thousands of visitors a year.

Holding an AK-47 rifle, a schoolgirl stands guard at a World War II monument in Irkutsk, Siberia. Most Soviet children belong to the Young Pioneers — described in their charter as "convinced fighters for the Communist Party cause."

THE OMNIPOTENT STATE

The state, according to Karl Marx, is an instrument of oppression. He envisaged a society in which workers and peasants would manage their own factories and land, and the state would "wither away." More than half a century after Marx's followers won control of the Russian Empire, that has yet to happen. The state in the U.S.S.R. is more powerful and authoritarian than in any other nation.

Supported by an immense military machine and an omnipresent internal-security apparatus, the Kremlin seeks to control every aspect of life. Inevitably, the state's reach exceeds its grasp. Underground factories and black markets make up a *nalevo* — "on the left" — economy challenging the official one. Dissident publications and bold demonstrations of defiance sporadically oppose official policies.

Nevertheless, the state is the heart, if not the soul, of the Soviet Union, and the power behind the state is the Communist Party. At every level, the party makes or affects all policy decisions; government functionaries carry them out. In the Army, party "political officers" are assigned to each commander (usually a party member himself) to ensure implementation of party policy.

Party members number about 18 million, almost 10 per cent of the adult population. They are recruited from all segments of Soviet society. Membership usually ensures rapid career advancement and is all but essential for anyone with political ambitions. It demands great agility in following twists in the party line. It also entails devoting much time to meetings and administrative duties, as well as paying the dues (up to 3 per cent of salary for top officials) that support all party functions.

All members belong to one of about 400,000 primary party organizations based at their workplaces. From there the party pyramids through city, district, regional and republic levels to the Central Committee, made up of perhaps 500 members elected every five years to represent all parts of the U.S.S.R. At the apex are the Secretariat, which serves as the party's general staff; and the Politburo, which meets weekly to make the party's, and hence the nation's, policy decisions. One man, the party's General Secretary, chairs the Politburo and also the Secretariat. He is first among equals, chief steward of power, *the* Soviet leader.

From this apex of power — whose pattern recurs in miniature at every level of Soviet society — the party runs the nation. It exerts its will through government structures organized like those in other countries but staffed in key positions by high party officials.

The executive branch of government, for example, is headed by the Council of Ministers — which numbers about 100 members, including chiefs of ministries, agencies and commissions, along with the premiers of the 15 union republics. The chairman of the Council is the Soviet Premier, technically the head of government. In fact, the Premier, along with the most important other Cabinet members, such as the Minister of Defense, derive their real power by virtue of seats on the party's Politburo. When Nikita Khrushchev was party leader, he chose to wear the additional hat of Premier.

The Council of Ministers is appointed by the nation's parliament, the Supreme Soviet, on the recommendation of its 39-member steering committee, the Presidium. The Supreme Soviet — and the subsidiary soviets at the republic and local levels — are elected by the citizens of the U.S.S.R. However, these elections are hardly free and open. Rather, they are examples of what the Russians wryly call *pokazuka*. Roughly translated, *pokazuka* means to make a show, to make things look different from reality. The process begins a few months before the balloting, with mass meetings to nominate candidates.

Typically, these meetings are stage-managed so that three people are nominated for a single seat in the Supreme Soviet, but only one of them — the one chosen for the post by the party secretary of the district — can be elected. After a suitable lapse of time, the dummy candidates graciously bow out, leaving only the one candidate. This political gavotte goes on all over the country in such a manner that the nominations will produce a balanced, predetermined slate: About a third of the 1,500 candidates will be important party functionaries, government ministers, and top military and police officers; the remainder will provide token representation for various ethnic groups, occupations and even ages.

Although each candidate runs unopposed, an enormous election campaign is mounted. Everyone 18 and over is

6

eligible to cast a ballot, and as much as 5 per cent of the electorate may be mobilized by the government to make sure that everyone does. These electioneers go door-to-door to campaign, to transport voters to the polls — where refreshments are often served — and to carry portable ballot boxes to hospitals.

The voter then faces a ballot with the single name on it. Dropping that ballot in the box constitutes a "yes" vote. To cast a "no" ballot — write-ins are forbidden — the voter must strike out the name. However, the voters — at least at the local level — are not sheep and they occasionally refuse to react as they are supposed to. If an incompetent party secretary nominates someone who is widely disliked, there sometimes are so many "no" votes that the official candidate is defeated. Then a new candidate and a new election (and generally a new party secretary) are called for.

What counts for the Soviets is getting out the vote, and the official statistics invariably vindicate the effort as a success. After the 1982 local elections, for example, *Pravda* reported that 99.98 per cent of the nation's 177,995,382 eligible voters turned out. It is all *pokazuka*, of course. Elections are an elaborate charade intended to demonstrate virtually unanimous support for the leadership and its policies.

The climb to the top of the party ladder is never easy. An instructive, if extreme, example is the career of Nikita Khrushchev. In 1915, as a 21-year-old metalworker in the Ukraine, Khrushchev began reading the party's propaganda. By 1917 he was a labor organizer, and the next year, shortly after the Revolution, he joined the party.

During the civil war that followed the Revolution, he served as a political commissar in the Red Army, watching

for treasonous tendencies among the officers who had been recruited from the old Imperial Army. Soon after the War he became a full-time party *apparatchik* (essentially, a party civil servant) and his enthusiasm quickly earned the regard of Ukrainian party bosses who were close to Stalin. Khrushchev's zealous support of Stalin in a series of bitter intraparty disputes enhanced his position, and when he took a leave from his party job in 1929 to study at Moscow's Industrial Academy, the party hierarchy continued to follow his progress.

At the academy, he quickly took over the local party committee and turned what had been a troublesome hotbed of dissidents into a bastion of Stalinist orthodoxy. Perhaps more important, he struck up a friendship with a classmate at the Academy, Nadezhda Alliluyeva — Stalin's wife. In 1932, he left the academy before graduating, to become Second Secretary of the party's Moscow Committee. Three years later he was promoted to First Secretary, an office that enabled him to build a power base by naming his supporters to key posts; three years after that he became First Secretary for the Ukraine, and by

1939 he was a member of the Politburo. His position in the Ukraine not only alowed him to broaden his power base with supporters there but also kept him out of Moscow from 1938 to 1949; his distance from the Kremlin may have saved him from the fate that befell many an erstwhile Stalin loyalist caught in that capricious leader's purges of the party hierarchy. Once back in Moscow, Khrushchev managed to stay in Stalin's good graces, and he was thus able to fill key party jobs with officials loyal to him. His skill in gaining powerful supporters served him well when Stalin died in 1953. Over the next few months, Khrushchev mobilized allies to vote down his rivals in the party's upper echelons, and won for himself the top job.

He held the post for 11 years, but he also made powerful enemies inside the party, with a vigorous campaign of de-Stalinization and reorganization of party structure. Many upper-level apparatchiks saw their careers threatened and they turned against him, finally ousting him from power at a meeting of the Central Committee in 1964.

However risky and arduous the climb, those who make it up the party

Carrying a bag bulging with luxuries from a Beriozka Gastronom in Moscow, designated for foreigners, a high official enters his limousine. Its license plate identifies it as a Central Committee car.

DUAL ROLES OF PARTY AND GOVERNMENT

The Communist Party and the Soviet government are intertwined, linking most closely in shared control over the armed forces. The party proposes, the government disposes. At the head of the party is the General Secretary, the individual most powerful in the Soviet Union. He presides at the weekly meetings of the Politburo, the major policy-making body of the party and, in effect of the country. A third of its members hold key posts in both government and party.

The General Secretary also heads the Secretariat, which handles day-to-day problems of the party. In addition, he presides over meetings of the Central Committee. This prestigious group gathers twice a year to review policies set by the Politburo.

While the party has one head, the government has two: the Premier and the President (at times, the party Secretary General has also held one or the other of these posts). The Premier, the country's chief executive officer, oversees the Presidium, a cabinet-like body; he also presides over the Council of Ministers, which is made up of the chiefs of 100 departments and agencies.

The President is chairman of the rubber-stamp parliament, the Supreme Soviet, which holds three- or four-day sessions twice a year to approve legislation and the national budget. The Supreme Soviet has its own Presidium, which operates as its steering committee between sessions.

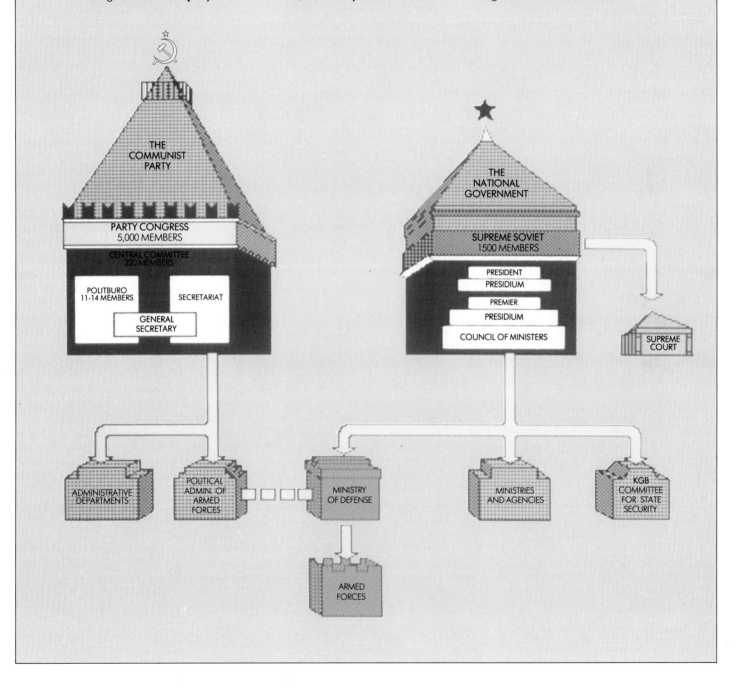

ladder join a privileged class of perhaps a million people that also includes prominent writers, scientists, artists, athletes, military officers and government officials. They are the movers and shakers in Soviet society and, like leaders everywhere, they expect to enjoy large salaries and special privileges.

For many of these *nachalstvo* — bosses — the most prized perquisite is foreign travel. At home they have access to spacious city apartments as well

as country dachas, to private cars or even limousines, and to a network of exclusive hospitals and clinics. They can shop at special stores that sell rare imported and domestic items — French Cognac or just fresh fruit — as well as ordinary groceries at low prices.

These perquisites are bestowed according to rank. A former bureaucrat recalls that even in the snack bars of the Kremlin, "there is a hierarchy: The higher the floor, the lower the prices

and the wider and more luxurious the range of merchandise." American cigarettes and Scotch whisky, for example, are reserved for the top floors.

Though the perquisites of power cannot be directly bequeathed to the next generation, the elite is self-perpetuating. Members use their influence to arrange good educations and important jobs for sons and daughters.

The fact that privileges are accorded the *nachalstvo* is acknowledged, even though it contradicts the egalitarian ideal of Marxism: "From each according to his ability, to each according to his need." That ideal is held as a goal for the future. Meanwhile, people get rewards for their work, as in other social systems. Said Stalin in 1931: "Only people unacquainted with Marxism can have the primitive notion that the Russian Bolsheviks want to pool all wealth and then share it out equally."

Thus today, as in the old Russian Em-

pire, the nation is ruled from above by an autocratic elite. A young Western politician who visited there once likened the Soviet system to "one big corporation — U.S.S.R., Incorporated." The image is apt, for the system, like a corporation, is responsible for everything within its domain. Moreover, its most important business is indeed business. And in many respects it adheres to procedures typical of corporations.

From a highly centralized bureaucracy in Moscow, the state runs the economy. With a few exceptions — collective farms, artisans' workshops, and some stores and services run as cooperatives — the nation's capital assets are state-owned and -operated. Revenues from state enterprises, plus sales taxes on manufactured goods and a low personal income tax, are the state's income; its expenditures finance the whole economy, and the budget is always balanced.

The basic instrument through which the state controls the economy is known simply as the Plan, with a capital P. It is not unlike a Brobdingnagian version of the plan of a large, diversified corporation, a complex of plans encompassing all state enterprises. It sets production targets, fixes prices and allocates raw materials and labor. The Plan tells a steel mill how many tons to produce, tells a restaurant how many meals to serve and even stipulates how many court cases a lawyer must try.

The Plan emanates from the State Planning Commission — Gosplan — on the basis of priorities set by the Politburo. Once it has been rubber-stamped by the parliament, the Plan carries the force of law. "We live under a tyranny," a Soviet intellectual once remarked, "the tyranny of the Plan."

The various levels of the Plan cover periods ranging from a month to five

Despite sporadic campaigns to punish laziness, many Soviet workers, like this napping maintenance man, loaf on the job. Foreign observers and the Soviets themselves blame such idleness for the ills of the nation's economy.

ALL IN THE FAMILY, RUSSIAN STYLE

Workers at the Leninsky plant remain in the factory orbit both on and off the job, cosseted by the services their workplace provides.

In the year 1903, an official inspecting a Russian sugar factory was dismayed to find the workers living in huge, barracks-like dormitories. Thinking to improve their lot by providing them with a modicum of privacy, he proposed that partitions be erected between their cots — only to be met with a storm of objections from the workers. "Are we cattle, that we should be cooped up in stalls?" they protested.

This favoring of proximity over privacy survives undiminished among the workers of the 1980s — and Soviet authorities make the most of it. People who work together — party officials, military officers, newspaper editors, farm hands or factory machinists — are made to feel that they are members of a family, responsible for one another, dependent on one another and secure in their shared lives. A workplace typically provides employees with everything they need for their daily lives: residences, child-care centers, medical services, theaters and vacation accommodations. Not all workplaces offer services of equal quality, but the services are always better than those available in the outer world. They go with the job and end when the job ends. It is security not from cradle to grave, but from cradle to workbench.

This collective living can be seen at its idealized best at the Leninsky Komsomol Automobile Plant in Moscow *(above)*, known as AZLK for its Russian initials. A showplace displaying Soviet-style industry as it is meant to be seen, the plant is the country's second-largest manufacturer of passenger vehicles, producing 200,000 Moskvich compact cars a year. AZLK provides its several thousand workers with necessities, comforts and amusements, including apartment houses a bus ride away from the plant *(page 144)*, nurseries, clinics and a "Palace of Culture" that serves up entertainment to fill leisure hours.

Near a cluster of factory-sponsored apartment houses, workers await a bus.

Children of Leninsky plant employees play in a toy-filled day-care center.

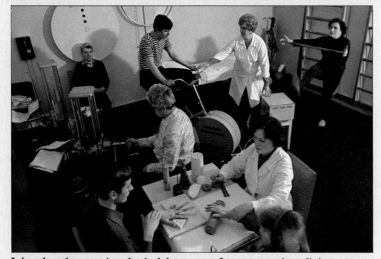
Injured workers receive physical therapy at a factory outpatient clinic.

For a nominal fee that is scaled to their wages, AZLK's working parents can place their children in one of 16 nurseries and kindergartens. Children are eligible for care in a nursery when they are only three months old; about 25 per cent of Soviet infants under the age of two spend eight to 12 hours a day in collective nurseries. However, some mothers and even some Soviet child psychologists object to such early separation of mother and baby; most women take advantage of the liberal maternity leave — a year off, including four months at full pay — to stay home and care for their infants themselves.

The daily regimen at the child-care center at AZLK — or anywhere else — is determined in Moscow and transmitted by handbook to teachers throughout the land. The authorities do not stint on facilities. One Western correspondent noted that even in farm collectives, which are less sophisticated than AZLK, "the nursery was often the brightest and certainly the cleanest spot on the premises, an obligatory stop on the official tour of the farm because the powers-that-be were so proud of it."

Children generally get top priority for fresh food and vitamins, as well as medical supervision. Health care for their elders is also provided by the workplace. Prestigious institutions such as the Academy of Sciences and the Bolshoi Ballet have special hospitals to serve their own members. Elsewhere, medical care is likely to be more routine. Workers may be lined up, hundreds at a time, for physical check-ups; the procedure consists of the doctor's walking down the line, asking each person in turn for complaints.

The AZLK factory provides more than an army-style sick call. It maintains eight medical stations in those of its shops where accidents are likely, as well as an outpatient clinic that provides continuing therapy for injured

At a well-stocked supermarket located near the factory gate, a young couple selects tea from a bin.

workers. A patient who needs medicines can buy them at a factory dispensary.

The factory also lends a helping hand with food to ensure that the employed eat well, even if others do not. Most staples are readily available, most of the time, in state stores, but more desirable fare may be hard to find. If the markets run short of such Russian favorites as sausage, cheese and canned fish, the factories are often able to get special consignments. When they do, foremen pass the word that the foods are available, and the workers can line up to buy allotments to take home.

The enveloping arm of the workplace is perhaps most conspicuous in arrangements for leisure activities. Sports, crafts and the performing arts are accessible to Soviet citizens practically everywhere, together with free instruction in arts and crafts.

Such activities are well attended. The AZLK Palace of Culture, on the factory premises, includes a motion picture theater, a 1,200-seat auditorium for amateur theatrical productions, a lending library, no fewer than 24 classes for folk dance alone, and still others for ballet and gymnastics. In that, it is not unique; factories in Minsk, Togliatti, Gorky, and perhaps half a dozen other cities have facilities as exten-

Backs to a bulletin board announcing shows and classes, three factory employees critique a painting in progress.

Workers swim in a 50-meter pool at a sports complex that also houses a skating rink, a gym and a stadium.

Two workers display their acting skills onstage at the Palace of Culture, where amateur theater productions go on year-round.

sive, and even small work organizations make some provisions for cultural activities.

Such palaces of culture arrange, through the unions, for vacation accommodations that range from camping tents in the mountains to hotel rooms on the Baltic. When workers take time off, they take it together.

The ubiquity of their fellow workers gives the Russians what they call "elbow feeling," by which they mean a sense of friends at their elbows, ever ready with support — in short, security. "We're living well," Russians like to tell Western visitors. And for their well-being they credit their government and the employers — also part of the state — that regard them as all of a family.

Ironically, the one group of citizens for whom no one brings news of special sausage consignments are those who are most apt to miss food delicacies: the elderly. When Soviet citizens leave the work force, they go with pensions — but for elbow feeling they must look to their kin. Collective welfare is for those who produce in the workplace.

6

years and are tailored to each enterprise. Westerners are familiar with the national Five-Year Plans, promulgated to set goals for economic development. Stalin launched the first Five-Year Plan in 1928. He chose that unit of time because it would cover the usual cycle of good and bad harvests and because back then it took that long to build major industrial plants.

The first Five-Year Plan gave top priority to the development of heavy industry such as steelmaking, mining and the manufacture of machine tools. It and the following Plans, which had similar priorities, achieved spectacular successes. Their marshaling of the nation's enormous labor force and bountiful natural resources transformed a peasant-based economy into a modern industrial state. Today, the Soviet Union ranks second only to the United States in overall industrial output and is first in steelmaking, traditionally an index of basic economic power. Moreover, in spite of the low priority the Plans have generally given to consumer goods, such production has increased enough to improve the quality of life in the Soviet Union. There has been comparatively little inflation, and for all the unequal allocation of privileges according to rank, Soviet society nevertheless shows a remarkable degree of economic equality, the direct result of the government's policy of standard wages.

The ability of this highly centralized economy to concentrate its resources is sometimes awesome. Consider, for example, the "hero project" that is the centerpiece for each Five-Year Plan, serving as a showcase of Soviet industrial might to the world and a source of pride to the nation's own citizens.

During the early 1970s, the hero project was construction of a mammoth

SOVIET FIRSTS IN SPACE

Soviet successes in space have been spectacular, as this list attests. But there have been failures, too. Several — costing the lives of four cosmonauts — marred development of the *Soyuz* craft

(above), designed for missions to space stations. Efforts to land men on the moon also apparently ended in frustration; Western observers believe three launches either failed or were aborted.

Oct.	1957	**SPUTNIK 1**	First artificial earth satellite launched
Nov.	1957	**SPUTNIK 2**	First satellite to collect biological data; carried dog Laika
Sep.	1959	**LUNA 2**	First lunar probe to hit the moon
Oct.	1959	**LUNA 3**	First photographs of far side of the moon
Apr.	1961	**VOSTOK 1**	First manned orbital flight (Cosmonaut Yuri Gagarin)
June	1963	**VOSTOK 6**	First woman in space (Cosmonaut Valentina Tereshkova)
Oct.	1964	**VOSKHOD 1**	First three-man orbital flight
Mar.	1965	**VOSKHOD 2**	First space walk, lasting 20 minutes (Cosmonaut Alexei A. Leonov)
Jan.	1966	**LUNA 9**	First soft landing of a probe on the moon
Oct.	1967	**KOSMOS 186** **KOSMOS 188**	First automatic rendezvous and docking of satellites
Jan.	1969	**SOYUZ 4** **SOYUZ 5**	First link-up of two manned vehicles and transfer of crew
Oct.	1969	**SOYUZ 6**	First triple launch of manned ships
Nov.	1970	**LUNA 17**	First robot vehicle on the moon
Apr.	1971	**SALYUT 1**	First prototype of manned space station launched
July	1975	**APOLLO/SOYUZ JOINT PROJECT**	First international rendezvous and docking in space by U.S. and Soviet crews; aimed at developing a space rescue capability
Jan.	1978	**SOYUZ 27**	First triple docking in space
Aug.	1984	**SOYUZ T-10/11**	Record of 237 days living in space

truck factory on the Kama River, about 600 miles east of Moscow, near the Ural Mountains. There, at a cost of more than five billion dollars, Soviet engineers created from windswept fields of rye the world's largest self-contained manufacturing plant. Capable of producing 150,000 heavy vehicles a year virtually from scratch, the 23-square-mile complex is not merely an assembly plant; it has its own foundries and forges as well, and accommodates its 70,000 workers in a satellite city.

The latest hero project, the Baikal-Amur Mainline (BAM), is even more ambitious *(pages 58-65):* a 2,000-mile-long railroad through the remote and mountainous reaches of eastern Siberia, strategically located several hundred miles north of the original Trans-Siberian Railroad and linking up with Pacific ports.

Much of the Soviet Union's economic success rests on a broad foundation of scientific and technological research. In size, the Soviet scientific establishment is without equal. One and a half million researchers with degrees in science — one fourth of all such specialists in the world — are organized in a nationwide network of 3,000 institutes and in thousands of experimental laboratories and field stations.

At least half of this network comes under the direct jurisdiction of Moscow's Academy of Sciences, which also operates a special Siberian section at Akademgorodok, or Academic City, a suburb of Novosibirsk in central Siberia. This model community houses 60,000 people and contains more than 40 individual research institutes staffed by 3,000 scientists. Like scientific workers everywhere in the U.S.S.R., they are granted high salaries and opportunities for travel abroad. Akademgorodok of-

fers another plum — housing that is, by Soviet standards, luxurious.

By rewarding scientists with perquisites and prestige, the Soviet Union has attracted a high proportion of its ablest youth into the scientific establishment. And by carefully focusing their efforts, that establishment has achieved huge successes. Beginning in 1957, Soviet rocket specialists launched a series of space explorations that stunned the world: *Sputnik I*, the first artificial satellite, followed in 1959 by the first unmanned probe of the moon and in 1961 by the first manned orbital flight.

Two Nobel Prize-winning Soviet physicists, Andrei Sakharov and Igor Tamm, developed in the 1950s a theoretical basis for a device — the Tokamak — that promises safe, waste-free power from nuclear fusion; 10 years later another team of Soviet physicists built the first of these machines. At about the same time, yet another team was pioneering laser technology.

On a more immediately practical level the record is mixed. Soviet science and engineering have turned out many inventions now used in the West, including a surgical stapling gun, a pneumatic underground punch called a "hole hog" and a technique for turning coal into coal gas underground.

In many fields, however, Soviet technology lags. In mathematics, for example, Soviet theoreticians rank among the best in the world, but the nation is at least a decade behind the West in development and application of computers. In most Soviet offices and stores, calculations are still done with the ancient abacus. On average the U.S.S.R. imports 14 times as much machinery and equipment from the West as it exports to the West. When an auto plant was built in the 1970s, all the machin-

ery and equipment came from Italy.

Such failings affect civilian technology more than the military. The bulk of the nation's investment in scientific research is poured into its mammoth military effort. Probably $1/8$ of the Soviet gross national product (or GNP, the value of all goods and services produced in a given year) goes to the military. Israel, the biggest spender on defense, devotes more than $1/4$ of its small GNP to that purpose; France spends about $1/25$, and the U.S. about $1/16$.

The result of the enormous Soviet expenditure is weaponry in staggering quantities. Moreover, the quality is relatively high — much higher than that of civilian products. A former worker in a Soviet armaments plant described the system: "Military officers sit in each factory — in the big factories, these are generals — and they operate with strict discipline. They are empowered to reject *brak* [substandard items], and they reject great quantities." If the *brak* has any civilian application — reject blankets, electrical switches, gasoline engines — much of it is then dumped onto the consumer market.

Some factories, making a single item, are subdivided into three sections: military, export and domestic civilian. They have separate work forces and assembly lines organized in a simple hierarchy: The military section has the most experienced and best-paid workers, the newest machinery, the most generous production schedules and the strictest quality control. The export section gets second best, and the civilian section is stuck with what is left. Commented one Western journalist, "The Soviet Union has been first in space, first in tanks and last in ladies' lingerie."

The low priority accorded civilian goods is only one reason they are often

6

shoddy and in short supply. A highly centralized, from-the-top-down command structure often proves unwieldy and inefficient. Soviet factory managers, like executives everywhere, resort to numerous stratagems in order to beat the system imposed from above.

A manager may understate actual production capacity, making certain his plant does not exceed the current quota by more than 1 or 2 per cent. Otherwise his targets will be raised. (Workers, too, must be careful not to be too productive or their individual piecework quotas could go up.) At the same time, the manager accumulates hidden reserves of raw materials and labor to fulfill the Plan despite equipment breakdowns or worker absenteeism and supply shortages. "If you want a two-hump camel," a Russian saying goes, "you must order a three-hump camel. The system will shave off the extra hump."

Whole carloads of materials are late or simply never show up. A Soviet newspaper once reported that only 70 per cent of the trees harvested ever reached lumber or pulp mills; the rest were presumably ruined or stolen — or never harvested in the first place.

Stealing from the state is so common that it is a rich source of Russian jokes:

"I think that we have the richest country in the world," says Ivan.

"Why?" asks Volodya.

"Because for 65 years everyone has been stealing from the state, and still there is something left to steal."

Shortages are a particular problem in the Soviet economy because the system is so rigidly interlocked. A producer who is unable to secure a needed commodity from the supplier assigned to him by the central Plan cannot simply turn to another supplier. Many enterprises seek self-sufficiency, producing their own manufacturing machinery. Two thirds of the national stock of machine tools is dispersed among factories that use them to make the machinery needed to manufacture their principal products. This dispersion helps eliminate some supply bottlenecks, but it breaks up what might otherwise be a concentrated, specialized machinery-production industry, and thus it adds to overall production inefficiency.

More ingenious managers do what their Western counterparts do. They make deals — but on a grand scale. How they get the things they need was described in a fictional — but true-to-life — account of the tribulations of a construction supervisor. In a book called *In Plain Russian,* by Vladimir Voinovich, the hero desperately needs linseed oil to thin paint that is to be used in a new apartment building. After fruitless appeals to the official supply chief, he tries to secure the oil through a complicated series of swaps with his fellow supervisors. He draws up a detailed list of supplies each one needs, and supplies each has to spare:

CONSTRUCTION SUPERVISOR	HAS	NEEDS
Filiminov	Linseed oil	Roofing iron
Limar	Dutch tiles	Window frames
Sidorkin	Roofing iron	Dutch tiles
Ermoshin	Window frames	Tiles
Me	Tiles	Linseed oil

"A complete strategic plan," he laments, "and all for one barrel of linseed oil." But it pays off. Eventually he gets two barrels for his trouble.

In spite of the inventiveness of such middle-level managers, bottlenecks persist, and they set a wildly erratic monthly rhythm of production. In practically every kind of industrial plant, the pace of the month's work tends to move forward in three distinct 10-day periods, described by one Soviet worker as *spyachka,* or "hibernation"; *goryachka,* or "hot time"; and *likhoradka,* "feverish frenzy" or "storming."

The first 10 days of *spyachka,* key supplies are usually missing, many workers are absent, and little gets done. During the *goryachka* middle 10 days, parts start dribbling in from suppliers and the pace picks up. Then, in the final 10 days, the rest of the supplies arrive, and the manager, his bonuses dependent on meeting the monthly quota, throws in hidden reserves of workers and puts everyone on overtime.

A typical factory may turn out 80 per cent of its monthly quota in those 10 days of *likhoradka* — storming. Goods are tagged with the date of production, and consumers try to shun anything made after the 20th of the month.

If storming and stratagems fail, the manager has one last resort for fulfilling the Plan: He falsifies his report. A poultry breeder from Central Asia told how his state farm met the daily target of 100,000 eggs — by writing off "30,000 to 40,000 eggs as if they had been broken and fed to the chickens, even though those eggs never existed."

Not surprisingly, the inability of the official economy to provide the goods and services people need has spawned a second, largely unofficial, economy to fill the gap. Operated by private entrepreneurs, this parallel economy is part legal, part illegal. Even the illegal part is winked at if it stays small.

Some professionals who work for the state, such as physicians, are permitted to moonlight at home. Workers on state and collective farms are allowed to cultivate small private gardens and sell their produce for whatever the market will bear. With these exceptions, pri-

DETENTE ON THE HIGH SEA

Putting aside political differences, the Union of Soviet Socialist Republics and the United States joined forces in 1976 in a surprising venture: They founded a profit-making business called Marine Resources. Today 21 Soviet ships like the one at left regularly enter the offshore waters of the United States and take on board fish that have been caught for them by American fishermen.

The company is owned fifty-fifty by the Bellingham Cold Storage company of Bellingham, Washington, and the Soviet Ministry of Fisheries. Every autumn, representatives of the two countries meet in Moscow, and there they go over figures projecting the availability of fish and the size of next season's market. Then, sometime in late January or early February, Soviet ships leave Siberian ports and rendezvous with American trawlers in the Bering Sea, in the Gulf of Alaska or off the Washington-Oregon coast. American observers live aboard the ships to monitor the size of the catch and to see that Soviet crews do not fish on their own while they are in American waters.

The ships are floating factories, equipped to sort, clean, and salt or freeze the catch that they receive from the American trawlers. Some of the larger factory ships — which can process more than 300 tons of fish a day — also double as service vessels, providing smaller ones with fuel, water and supplies. Fish deemed inedible for humans are reduced to fish meal for use as animal feed or fertilizer.

Once their lockers are full, the factory ships either transfer their cargo to other vessels for transport back to the U.S.S.R. or, at the season's end, deliver it there themselves. From the Siberian port of Nakhodka, Marine Resources distributes fish throughout the Soviet Union and to 16 other countries in Europe and Asia.

A Soviet ship hauls in fish caught for her by American fishermen in U.S. waters.

Pollock and hake crowd the deck before being hoisted into the hold for processing.

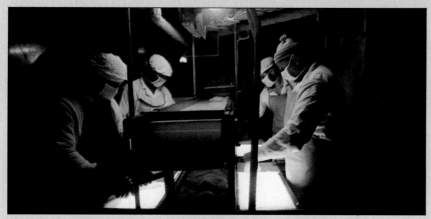
Below deck, surgically masked processors examine fish, checking for parasites.

151

6

vate enterprise is outside the law in the Soviet Union, and most of the second economy has to operate underground.

At its everyday level, this *nalevo* economy consists of exchanges of favors and services, moonlighting by plumbers and other craftworkers, and the private selling of scarce goods such as automobiles *(page 21)*. But *nalevo* manufacturing and retail sales can become big business, amounting to 10 per cent or more of the gross national product.

The mainstays of the underground economy are the ubiquitous *fartsovshchiki* — the black-market merchants. These merchants set up shop in cafes, on street corners or even in public toilets. The weekly magazine *Literaturnaya gazeta*, investigating the black market, once sent a reporter to the city of Krasnodar near the Black Sea with instructions to buy a toothbrush, soap, razor blades, shaving cream, underclothes, socks and writing paper. The reporter spent a day scouring the government stores and could not find a single item. Then he turned to the *fartsovshchiki* and quickly finished his shopping.

Some *fartsovshchiki* are officially acknowledged when the police feel compelled to act. A Lithuanian lawyer, Elizabeth Tyntareva, started small, peddling coveted articles such as sunglasses and women's wigs. Gradually she branched out into gold rings, watches, jeans and umbrellas, and developed a regular clientele among vacationers on the Baltic. By 1980, when she was arrested and sentenced to 12 years in prison, Tyntareva had four assistants and a mail-order service.

Many underground goods are smuggled in from the West or bought from foreigners who get them in *beriozki* — special government stores reserved for foreign tourists and diplomats. But surprising quantities of illicit consumer goods, ranging from sweaters to recordings of Western popular music, are made in the Soviet Union by the nation's own underground industries.

In these remarkable establishments, clandestine entrepreneurs literally use the machinery of the state to undercut the official economy. They operate under the same roofs and same names as the state-owned factories. And while the state factory produces under the government Plan, the factory-within-a-factory runs a second shift — with the same workers and same equipment — to make illicit goods in secret. The underground entrepreneur gets the supplies, pays the workers and reaps the profits — but uses capital investment unwittingly furnished by the state. And the officials who have looked the other way earn their share.

Says Konstantin Simis, a Soviet attorney who defended underground businessmen in dozens of court cases before he was forced into exile, such factories are centered in major cities such as Moscow, Odessa, Tbilisi and Riga. They are linked by an informal network of commercial and personal ties.

Among the remarkable underground entrepreneurs Simis met in his law practice were the three Glazenberg brothers. Like many others who go underground, the Glazenbergs are Jewish. Following their discharge from the Army after World War II, they were barred from legitimate careers in the government or party by Stalin's anti-Semitism. So, using their discharge bonuses, they bribed their way into a factory making plastic shopping bags. By paying off the workers involved, they got them to exceed the factory's quota. Then, to keep them producing, they cut the workers in on the profits from the illegal sale of the extra bags.

The brothers prospered, and soon added other *nalevo* industries through handshake deals. To oversee their underground empire, which eventually included at least 10 factories that made not only shopping bags but handbags and imitation-leather jackets as well, the Glazenbergs formed a family board of directors. They hired a manager for each business and paid 500 to 1,000 rubles a month in bribes to the colluding director of each of the official factories that housed their operations.

Procuring supplies was harder. One source was the underground. The Glazenbergs arranged a network of illicit subcontractors: Clasps, buttons, labels all came from other *nalevo* factories.

But the main source for raw materials was the state itself. Whenever a new product was planned for one of the official factories, the Glazenbergs or their hired help would bribe the government technicians responsible for setting the standards for raw materials. The technicians would then inflate the estimates of quantities of materials needed to make the product; the resulting surplus went into the underground goods.

Marketing the products was simple at first for the Glazenbergs. They sold their illicit shopping bags through the same state store that carried the factory's officially produced bags, greasing the way by giving shop employees a one-third cut. Later, the brothers established a special marketing group who traveled the country and organized sales outlets in 64 towns and regions.

An enterprise this large was bound to come to the attention of a special police agency, the Department for Combating Misappropriation of Socialist Property. In fact, the DCMSP had a complete dossier on the Glazenbergs. This did not overly concern the brothers, since they were bribing key officials; but then a low-ranking bureaucrat tipped off a reporter at *Izvestia*, who began sifting through the few papers the high officials felt obliged to let him see.

To cover up the mess, the officials soon removed the dossier from their files and warned the Glazenbergs so they would have time to secrete their money and valuables. But they concluded that some legal action could not be avoided: One of the brothers would have to be sacrificed. Lazar Glazenberg, the youngest, was tried, convicted and sentenced to 15 years in a labor camp, where he died seven years later.

Lazar was chosen as the sacrificial example largely because of his flamboyant life style. Most underground entrepreneurs tend to avoid conspicuous consumption so as not to attract attention to themselves. Some manage to find legal sources of income to explain whatever spending they dare to do. A big winner in the government lottery may be paid two or three times his winnings to turn over his lucky ticket to the *nalevo* magnate. Others of the underground rich convert their rubles into dollars, precious stones and gold, and hide these valuables, hoarding wealth that they may never spend.

For many, unable to use much of their *nalevo* income on anything else, the main indulgence is gambling. At any of several secret salons in the major cities, they can show their wealth freely. One such salon was maintained during the 1970s in the Moscow apartment of Elizabeth Mirkien, a handsome woman whose husband was in prison for illicit economic activities. Here, until the authorities clamped down, middle-aged businessmen could enjoy good food and drink, play cards and roulette and,

for the evening at least, feel the euphoria of spending recklessly money they had risked so much to accumulate.

In economic matters, only extremes such as the cases of the Mirkiens and the Glazenburgs provoke the government to exercise its right to regulate all facets of life. In other matters it is less tolerant. Political views are subject to stringent control, and deviations from the party line put the dissenter at grave risk. Although the Soviet Constitution guarantees freedom of expression and many other rights, it also forbids their exercise if deemed detrimental to "the interest of society or the state," and it flatly bans anti-Soviet agitation.

To watch over political behavior, the state maintains a ministerial-level police agency, the Committee for State Security — better known by its initials in Russian, KGB. The KGB employs an estimated 700,000 agents for domestic surveillance; one of every 250 adult Soviet citizens may thus be a KGB operative. Many of them are assigned to the personnel departments of factories, government agencies and universities.

Full-time agents are supplemented by tens of thousands of casual workers paid by the KGB as informers and known contemptuously by most Russians as *stukachi*, or squealers. In Moscow apartment buildings, for example, residents take for granted that the little old lady who runs the elevator is a KGB informer, paid to report on suspicious events such as a visit by a foreigner.

Anyone arrested for suspected subversion faces a justice system heavily weighted toward the interests of the state. Consider, for example, the published account of the case of Nikolai, a young factory worker in the small town of Podolski, near Moscow. Nikolai was identified by fellow workers as the

painter of angry complaints on the wall of the plant: "Why is our pay so low?" "Why is there no meat in the stores?"

Nikolai was arrested and charged with "political hooliganism." The pretrial investigation was handled by the procurator — a state prosecutor with powers much broader than those of his Western counterparts. The procurator establishes guilt or innocence before any trial is held. The main purpose of the trial is to decide punishment.

Nikolai was brought before a People's Court, a judge and two people's assessors — rubber-stamp lay jurists chosen, like the judge, without opposition in local elections. Testimony followed a line agreed upon by Nikolai's defense attorney and the procurator: Nikolai was a drunkard who did not know what he was doing when he painted the graffiti. His lawyer hoped this line would mitigate the severity of the sentence. Nikolai got seven years' exile in a far corner of Siberia.

In Stalin's time, it might have been much worse. At the height of that reign of terror, citizens accused of political offenses were tortured into confessions, tried secretly by police tribunal and either executed or shipped off to living death in the infamous Gulag — the Soviet Union's vast network of labor camps. Alexander Solzhenitsyn, in his chronicle of the camps, *The Gulag Archipelago, 1918-1956,* graphically recounts the terror — starvation rations, endemic disease, brutal working conditions — and sardonically charts the kinds of people Stalin sent there:

And so in 1948, 1949, and 1950 there flowed past:
● *Alleged spies (ten years earlier they had been German and Japanese, now they were Anglo-American).*

6

A recently laid section of the 2,900-mile-long Siberian natural-gas pipeline snakes through the snowy taiga. Today the pipeline carries gas to Western Europe, running from the heart of Siberia to the Czech border.

● *Believers (this wave non-Orthodox for the most part).*

● *Just plain ordinary thinking people (and students, with particular severity) who had not been sufficiently scared away from the West. It was fashionable to charge them with:*

● *VAT — Praise of American Technology*

● *VAD — Praise of American Democracy; and*

● *PZ — Toadyism Toward the West.*

As many as 20 million people may have been sent to these camps — three million are said to have died in just one of them, the huge complex at Kolyma in northeastern Siberia, where the principal labor is gold mining and the winter cold almost unbearable.

Some of the worst abuses disappeared after Stalin's death. But the camps remain. They contain most of the two million people currently im-

prisoned in the Soviet Union, a population that is believed to include 10,000 dissidents jailed for expressing their religious or political convictions.

A punishment that many view as worse than the Gulag is the practice of committing vocal dissenters to mental institutions. An estimated 1,000 dissidents have been forcibly confined to hospitals, diagnosed as schizophrenics.

One such case is that of Pyotr Grigorenko, a former Red Army general and war hero. His symptom of mental illness was outspokenness in behalf of the Crimean Tartars who want to return to the homeland from which they were expelled during World War II as suspected Nazi collaborators. When Grigorenko was asked by a psychiatrist, "Why did you protest?" his answer — "I couldn't breathe" — then became evidence of his alleged psychopathology. He was twice confined to asylums and finally, in 1978, permitted to emigrate in the West. There he was reexamined by a team of medical and mental-health specialists. "We concluded that Grigorenko was not mentally ill when we examined him," wrote Dr. Walter Reich, a member of the team, "and had probably not been mentally ill when the Soviet examiners had said he was."

Dr. Reich believes that Soviet psychiatrists are under pressure to diagnose mental illness in dissidents, both to avoid potentially embarrassing public trials and to discredit dissent as the product of sick minds. And a dutiful Soviet bureaucrat is likely to have perfectly sincere doubts about the mental state of any vocal dissident. After all, points out Dr. Reich, dissent is by definition deviant behavior, and in the Soviet Union it is known to be dangerous.

Concerned as they are about dissent and subversion at home, Soviet leaders

seem even more worried about threats from abroad. Their country's history of vulnerability to invaders, from Genghis Khan to Napoleon to Hitler, has left a legacy of almost paranoid wariness. Even in periods of "peaceful coexistence" and "détente," the government has sought to surround the nation with friendly buffer nations. Russia's once-exposed western border, for example, is now shielded not only by the Ukrainian, Belorussian and Baltic Republics that are integrated into the U.S.S.R., but also by a string of satellite states from Poland to Rumania.

The Soviet leadership will not countenance political activity in these buffers that might weaken their allegiance to Moscow — as it has repeatedly shown by intervening in the affairs of East Germany (1953), Hungary (1956), Czechoslovakia (1968), Afghanistan (1979) and Poland (1980). Outside these areas, the U.S.S.R. has used its role as world leader in Marxist Communism to strengthen its international position, serving as both ideological beacon and source of practical aid to other countries — or to political factions within the countries.

Yet however repressive their government may be, the people of the Soviet Union love their country. They have endured revolution and wars together; they have seen friends and relatives dragged off to labor camps, many never to return; they have put up with a system that promises far more than it can deliver. If they have grown cynical in the process, they have not lost a sense of themselves as being special, a people whom suffering has set apart, inhabitants of a land that a half century ago was a backward nation and now, by dint of their labor, is the undisputed power in its corner of the globe.

Sergei Batovrin, the leader of a pacifist group, stares from the window of a psychiatric hospital where he was held for a month. Such confinement is the fate of many dissidents.

ACKNOWLEDGMENTS

The index for this book was prepared by Barbara L. Klein. For their help with this volume, the editors also wish to thank: Vasily Aksyonov, Goucher College, Towson, Md.; Cyril E. Black, Princeton University, Center of International Studies, Princeton, N.J.; James E. Cole, Economic Research Service, U.S. Department of Agriculture, Washington, D.C.; Frederick Crory, U.S. Army Cold Regions Research and Engineering Laboratory, Hanover, N.H.; Murray Feshbach, Kennedy Institute of Ethics, Georgetown University, Washington, D.C.; Steven A. Grant, U.S.I.C.A., Washington, D.C.; Dmitry Grigorieff, Georgetown University, Washington, D.C.; George W. Hoffman, Department of Geography, The University of Texas, Austin, Tex.; Deborah A. Kaple, Wharton Econometric Forecasting Associates, Washington, D.C.; John W. Kiser, Kiser Research, Inc., Washington, D.C.; Gail Lapidus, Kennan Institute for Advanced Studies, Woodrow Wilson International Center for Scholars, Washington, D.C.; Sander H. Lee, Howard University, Washington, D.C.; Fairy von Lilienfeld, Institute of History and Theology of the Christian East, School of Theology, University of Erlangen/Nürnberg, West Germany; Nancy Lubin, Office of Technology Assessment, U.S. Congress, Washington, D.C.; Paul E. Lydolph, Department of Geography, University of Wisconsin, Milwaukee, Wis.; Dmitry Mikheyev, Arlington, Va.; Henry Morton, Queens College, Flushing, N.Y.; Victor Mote, University of Houston, Tex.; Bruce W. Nelan, *Time*, Washington, D.C.; Rose Nelan, Fairfax, Va.; David E. Powell, Russian Research Center, Harvard University, Cambridge, Mass.; Elisavietta Artanoff Ritchie, Washington, D.C.; Richard M. Robin, George Washington University, Washington, D.C.; Vladimir G. Treml, Duke University, Durham, N.C.; Adam B. Ulam, Russian Research Center, Harvard University, Cambridge, Mass.; Jan Vaňous, Wharton Econometric Forecasting Associates, Washington, D.C. These sources were particularly useful in the preparation of this volume: "Russia's Underground Millionaires" by Konstantin Simis, *Fortune*, June 29, 1981; and *Inside Russian Medicine* by William A. Knaus, Everest House/Dodd, Mead & Co., Inc., 1981. The editors are also indebted to the following quoted sources: *Involuntary Journey to Siberia* by Andrei Amalrik by permission of Harcourt Brace Jovanovich, Inc. Fyodor Dostoyevsky: *The Devils* trans. David Magarshack (Penguin Classics, Revised edition 1971). Fyodor Dostoyevsky: *Crime & Punishment* trans. David Magarshack (Penguin Classics 1966). "A Letter from Moscow" by Joseph Kraft in the *New Yorker*. *Russian Journal* by Andrea Lee by permission of Random House, Inc. *The Romanovs* by W. Bruce Lincoln. A Dial Press Book by permission of Doubleday & Co., Inc. *Peter the Great: His Life and His World* by Robert K. Massie by permission of Alfred A. Knopf, Inc. *Land of the Firebird: The Beauty of Old Russia* by Suzanne Massie by permission of Simon and Schuster, Inc. *Lectures on Russian Literature* by Vladimir Nabokov translated and reprinted by permission of Harcourt Brace Jovanovich, Inc. *U.S.S.R.: The Corrupt Society* by Konstantin Simis by permission of Simon and Schuster, Inc. *In Plain Russian* by Vladimir Voinovich by permission of Farrar, Straus and Giroux, Inc.

BIBLIOGRAPHY

BOOKS

Akhmatova, Anna, *Poems of Anna Akhmatova*. Atlantic Monthly Press, Little, Brown, 1973.

Amalrik, Andrei, *Involuntary Journey to Siberia*. Harcourt Brace Jovanovich, 1970.

Barrett, David B., *World Christian Encyclopedia*. London: Oxford University Press, 1982.

Berlin, Isaiah, *Russian Thinkers*. Viking, 1978.

Berliner, Joseph, *Innovation Decision in Soviet Industry*. Massachusetts Institute of Technology Press, 1976.

Billington, James H., *The Icon and the Axe*. Vintage, 1970.

Brine, Jenny, Maureen Perrie and Andrew Sutton, eds., *Home, School and Leisure in the Soviet Union*. George Allen & Unwin, 1980.

Bronfenbrenner, Urie, *Two Worlds of Childhood, U.S. and U.S.S.R.* Russell Sage, 1970.

Brown, Archie, John Fennell, Michael Kaser and H. T. Willetts, eds., *The Cambridge Encyclopedia of Russia and the Soviet Union*. Cambridge University Press, 1982.

Carrère d'Encausse, Helene, *Decline of an Empire*. Newsweek Books, 1980.

Center for International Studies, *Attitudes of Major Soviet Nationalities*. Massachusetts Institute of Technology Press, 1973.

Congressional Quarterly, *The Soviet Union*. Congressional Quarterly, Inc., 1982.

Connolly, Violet, *Siberia Today and Tomorrow*. Collins, 1975.

Conquest, Robert, ed., *Industrial Workers in the U.S.S.R.* Bodley Head, 1967.

Conquest, Robert, *V. I. Lenin*. Viking, 1972.

Crankshaw, Edward, ed., *Khrushchev Remembers*. Little, Brown, 1970.

Dewdney, John C., *A Geography of the Soviet Union*. Pergamon, 1979.

Dmytryshyn, Basil, *U.S.S.R.: A Concise History*. Charles Scribner's Sons, 1978.

Dornberg, John, *The Soviet Union Today*. Dial Press, 1976.

Dostoyevsky, Fyodor:
Crime and Punishment. Penguin, 1954.
The Devils. Penguin, 1957.

Dyck, H. W., *Boris Pasternak*. Twayne, 1972.

Ehre, Milton, ed., *The Theater of Nikolay Gogol*. Transl. by Früma Gottschalk. The University of Chicago Press, 1980.

Feshbach, Murray, *The Soviet Union: Population Trends and Dilemmas*. Population Reference Bureau, 1982.

Granick, David, *Red Executive*. Coser, Lewis & Powell, 1979.

Hecht, Leo, *The U.S.S.R. Today: Facts and Interpretations*. Scholasticus, 1982.

Hough, Jerry F., and Merle Fainsod, *How the Soviet Union is Governed*. Harvard University Press, 1979.

Jacoby, Susan, *Inside Soviet Schools*. Hill and Wang, 1974.

Joint Economic Committee, Congress of the

United States:
Soviet Economy in a Time of Change. Vols. I and II, Washington, D.C., 1979.
Soviet Economy in the 1980s: Problems and Prospects. Vols. I and II, Washington, D.C., 1982.

Kaiser, Robert G., *Russia, The People and the Power*. Pocket Books, 1976.

Kaiser, Robert G., and Hannah Jopling, *Russia From the Inside*. Dutton, 1980.

Keefe, Eugene K., et al., *Area Handbook for the Soviet Union*. U.S. Government Printing Office, 1971.

Knaus, William A., *Inside Russian Medicine*. Everest House, 1981.

Komarov, Boris, *The Destruction of Nature in the Soviet Union*. Transl. by Michel Vale and Joe Hollander. Sharpe, 1980.

Lapidus, Gail Warhofsky, *Women in Soviet Society*. University of California Press, 1978.

Lee, Andrea, *Russian Journal*. Random House, 1981.

Lincoln, W. Bruce, *The Romanovs*. Dial, 1981.

Lydolph, Paul E., *Geography of the U.S.S.R.* Misty Valley Publishing, 1979.

De Madariaga, Isabel, *Russia in the Age of Catherine the Great*. Yale University Press, 1981.

Mandelstam, Nadezhda, *Hope Against Hope*. Atheneum, 1970.

Massie, Robert K., *Peter the Great, His Life and World*. Ballantine, 1980.

Massie, Suzanne, *Land of the Firebird*. Simon and Schuster, 1980.

McDowell, Bart, *Journey Across Russia*. National Geographic, 1977.

Medish, Vadim, *The Soviet Union*. Prentice-Hall, 1981.

Mowat, Farley, *The Siberians*. Little, Brown, 1970.

Nabokov, Vladimir, *Lectures on Russian Literature*. Harcourt Brace Jovanovich, 1981.

Peskov, Vasili, *This Is My Native Land*. Moscow: Progress Publishers, 1976.

Pond, Elizabeth, *From the Yaroslavsky Station: Russia Perceived*. Universe Books, 1981.

Reavey, George, ed., *The New Russian Poets, 1953-1968*. October House, 1968.

Riasanovsky, Nicholas V., *A History of Russia*. Oxford University Press, 1977.

St. George, George, and the Editors of Time-Life Books, *Soviet Deserts and Mountains* (The World's Wild Places series) Time-Life Books, 1974.

Schecter, Jerrold and Leona; and Evelind, Steven, Kate, Doveen and Barnet, *An American Family in Moscow*. Little, Brown, 1975.

Silianoff, Eugene, *The Russians*. Little, Brown, 1980.

Simis, Konstantin, *U.S.S.R.: The Corrupt Society*. Simon and Schuster, 1982.

Smith, Hedrick, *The Russians*. Ballantine, 1976.

Solzhenitsyn, Aleksandr I., *The Gulag Archipelago*. Harper & Row, 1974.

Stanislavsky, Constantin, *My Life in Art*. Theatre Arts, 1952.

Tolstoy, Leo, *War and Peace*. Simon and Schuster, 1958.

Treadgold, Donald W., *Twentieth Century Russia*. Rand McNally, 1972.

Treml, Vladimir G., *Alcohol in the U.S.S.R., A Statistical Study*. Duke Press Policy Studies, 1982.

Troyat, Henri, *Pushkin*. Doubleday, 1970.

Ulam, Adam B.:
The Bolsheviks. Macmillan, 1965.
Russia's Failed Revolutions: From the Decembrists to the Dissidents. Basic Books, 1981.

Voinovich, Vladimir, *In Plain Russian*. Farrar, Straus & Giroux, 1979.

Wädekin, Karl-Eugen:
Agrarian Policies in Communist Europe. The Hague: Allanheld, Osmun, 1982.
The Private Sector in Soviet Agriculture. University of California Press, 1973.

Wallace, Robert, and the Editors of Time-Life Books, *Rise of Russia* (Great Ages of Man series). Time-Life Books, 1967.

Wilson, Edmund, *To the Finland Station*. Doubleday, 1953.

Yarmolinsky, Avrahm, *Two Centuries of Russian Verse*. Random House, 1966.

Yevtushenko, Yevgeni:
Bratsk Station and Other New Poems. Anchor, 1967.
Yevtushenko's Reader. Dutton, 1972.

PERIODICALS:

Crankshaw, Edward, "The Black Sheep of the Pokrovskoe." *New York Review of Books*, May 27, 1982.

Feifer, George:
"Russian Disorders." *Harper's*, Feb. 1981.
"Russian Winter." *Harper's*, Feb. 1982.

Greenfield, Marc, "Life Among the Russians." *New York Times Magazine*, Oct. 24, 1982.

Jordan, Robert Paul:
"The Proud Armenians," *National Geographic*, June 1978.
"Siberia's Empire Road, The River Ob." *National Geographic*, Feb. 1976.

Kraft, Joseph, "A Letter from Moscow." *New Yorker*, Jan. 31, 1983.

Lubin, Nancy, "Mullah and Commissar." *Geo*, June 1980.

Madison, Berenice, "The Problem That Won't Go Away." *Wilson Quarterly*, Autumn 1978.

Rythkeu, Yuri, "People of the Long Spring." *National Geographic*, Feb. 1983.

Simis, Konstantin, "Russia's Underground Millionaires." *Fortune*, June 29, 1981.

Time:
"Living Conveniently on the Left." June 23, 1980.
"OPEC Knuckles Under." Mar. 28, 1983.
"The Tough Search for Power." June 23, 1980.

Wädekin, Karl-Eugen, "Soviet Agriculture's Dependence on the West." *Foreign Affairs*, Spring 1982.

INDEX

Page numbers in italics refer to illustrations or illustrated text.

A

Agriculture, 47-48, *50-51, 53;* Central Asia, 73; collective farms, *12-13,* 50, 51, 53, *77;* illegal profits, 70-71
Akademgorodok, 149
Akhmadulina, Bella, and husband, *130-137*
Akhmatova, Anna, 128
Alcohol use, 27, 30
Alexander II, Tsar, 101, 103
Alexander Nevsky, 100
Alexandra, Tsarina, 103
Alexis (son of Peter the Great), 97-98
Alphabet, Cyrillic, *20*
Altai region, Siberia, *55*
Amalrik, Andrei, 53
Anna Karenina (Tolstoy), 123-124
Anti-Semitism, 79
Armenia and Armenians, 70, *71,* 72, *78;* churches, *49,* 70, *71;* rock festival, *129*
Army, Russian, reform of, 97
Art: avant-garde, 124, *125;* exhibit, *128;* Fabergé eggs, *120;* icons, *121;* modern, 124, *125;* studio, *130-131;* workers', *146*
Automobiles: production, *chart* 8, *143;* used, sale of, *21;* Leninsky Plant, *143-147*
Avant-garde art, 124, *125*
Azerbaijanians, 70; longevity, 72
AZLK (automobile plant), Moscow, *143-147*

B

Baikal, Lake, and area, 54-55
Baikal-Amur Mainline (BAM), *58-65,* 149
Ballet, 127; classes, *83, 127*
Baltic coast, *44-45*
Baltic peoples, 69-70
Balzac, Honoré de, 69
Banquets, historical, 93, *94-95*
Baptism, *113*
Barguzin sable, 54
Bath, steam *(bania),* 29-30
Batovrin, Sergei, *154*
Belorussia and Belorussians, 68, 69; garden plot, *53;* peat digging, *48;* state farm, *50-51*
Beriozka Gastronom, Moscow, *140*
Birth rates, 23, *chart* 76
Black-market merchants, 152
Bloody Sunday (1905), 103
Bolsheviks, 104, *105*
Boris Godunov (opera), 118, 126
Borodin, Alexander, 126-127
Brezhnev, Leonid I., *102*
Brodsky, Joseph, 128
Bronfenbrenner, Dr. Urie, 32
Bronze Horsemen, The (Pushkin), 119
Brothers Karamazov, The (Dostoyevsky), 120, 122
Buffer nations, 154
Buildings: construction workers, *80-81;* in permafrost region, 56. *See also* Housing
Bulganin, Nikolai, 23

C

Canal, Kara-Kum, 73
Cars: production, *chart* 8, *143;* used, *21*
Cathedral: St. Basil's, Moscow, *6-7,* 93, 100
Catherine II (the Great), Empress of Russia, 98-*99,* 101; crown of, 98, *99*
Caucasus region, peoples of, 70-72, *78*
Central Asian peoples, 67, 72-75, *73-75, 79*
Chagall, Marc, 124
Chekhov, Anton, 126
Cheptsov, Efim, painting by, *125*
Cherry Orchard, The (Chekhov), 117, 126
Chess, 28, *34*
Children and youth, *25,* 30, 32-33; baptism, *113;* day care, *144;* ethnic groups, *66, 78*
Children's World (store), Moscow, 19
Chukchis, 76
Churches, 106, *114-115;* Armenian, *49, 71;* St. Constantine and Helen, 114-115; *See also* Cathedral, Orthodox church
Circus, *23*
Cities, 16-17. *See also individual names*
Civil service, reorganization of, 97
Civil War (1918-1921), *102,* 104
Climate, *map* 13, 48, 56
Coal reserves, 46
Collective farms, *12-13,* 50, 51, 53, 77
Collectivization of reindeer herders, 78, *82*
Communist Party, 139, *chart* 141; Khrushchev in, 140; perquisites, members', *140,* 142
Composers, 126-127
Consumer goods, *chart* 14, 19-20; cars, *chart* 8, 21, *143;* illicit, 152; inferiority of, 25-26, 149; shopping procedure, 26, *38-39;* shortages, 26
Convents, *109*
Cossacks, 54; rebellion, 99
Creation stories, 71-72
Crime and Punishment (Dostoyevsky), 117, 120-122
Crimea: Catherine in, 99; Tartars, 78
Culture, 117; ballet, *83, 127;* 1890s-1930s, 127; factory workers, *146-147;* government control of, 117, 127-128, 129; music, 126-127; underground, 27. *See also* Art; Writers
Cyrillic alphabet, *20*

D

Dachas, 29, *34-35;* of writers, 131, *136*
Dams, effect of, 48
Dancing, *41;* ballet, *83, 127*
D'Anthès, Georges-Charles, 118
Day-care center, *144*
Dead Souls (Gogol), 120
Decembrist Revolt (1825), 103
Defense spending, 149
Demon, The (Lermontov), quoted, 119
Department stores, 19
Diderot, Denis, 98
Doctor Zhivago (Pasternak), 117, 128
Dostoyevsky, Feodor, 120-122
Dzerzhinsky Square, Moscow, 19

E

Easter, observances of, *106, 115*

Easter eggs, Fabergé, *120*
Economic control by state, 142, 148
Education, 32-33, *86*
Elections, 139-140
Elizabeth (daughter of Peter the Great), 98
Employment. *See* Work force
Energy sources, 46-47, *48;* Baikal, Lake, 54
Enlightenment philosophy, 98
Estonia and Estonians, 70; convent, *109*
Ethnic groups, 67-79; Armenians, 70, *71,* 72, *78;* Azerbaijanians, 70, 72; Baltic peoples, 69-70; Belorussians, 68, 69; birth rates, *chart* 76; Central Asia, *67,* 72-75, *79;* Georgians, *66,* 70, 71-72, *86-87, 90-91;* Kirgiz, 74; *map* 70; religion, *79;* Russians, *66,* 67-68, *91;* Russification, 78; Tadzhiks, 73-74; Tartars, 78; tensions between, 79; Turkomen, 74; Ukrainians, *52,* 68-69, *84-85,* 92; Uzbeks, 74, 75; Volga Germans, 78
Eugene Onegin (Pushkin), 127; quoted, 118
Examinations for universities, 32-33

F

Fabergé, Carl, Easter eggs by, *120*
Farming. *See* Agriculture
Fathers and Sons (Turgenev), 124, 126
Feshbach, Murray, 20
Films and movies, 28-29
Firebird, The (Stravinsky), 117
Fish and fishing, *41,* 48-49; Marine Resources operation, *151*
Five-Year Plans, 50, 148
Flax crop, failure of, 53
Folk art, window frames, *122-123*
Food, 19, *24,* 25, *75;* shopping for, 26, *38-39, 144-145*
Forests, 46
Fur industry, 54, *55;* model, *80*

G

Gambling salons, 153
Gas, natural, 46; pipeline, *155*
Gasanov, Shukur, 72
Gavrilova, Marina, 55-56
Georgians, *66,* 71-72, *86-87, 90-91*
Germans, Volga, 78
Glazenberg brothers, 152-153
Goat, *88-89*
Godunov, Boris, 95, 101
Gogol, Nikolai, 119-120
Gorky Park, Moscow, *34*
Government, Soviet, 139, *chart* 141; agriculture controlled by, *50-51,* 53; culture, control of, 117, 127-128, 129; economic control by, 142, 148; elections, 139-140; and ethnic groups, 78; local, 68; political behavior, 153-154
Great Purge (1930s), *102,* 105
Grigorenko, Pyotr, 154
Gulag Archipelago, The (Solzhenisyn), 129, 153
GUM department store, Moscow, 19

H

Hero projects, 148-149; Baikal-Amur Mainline, *58-65,* 149

History, 91-105; banquets, 93, *94-95;*
  Bolsheviks, 104, *105;* Catherine the Great, 98-
  99, 101; Central Asia, 73; chronology, *100-*
  102; Civil War, *102,* 104; collapse of Empire,
  103-104; conquerors, 91, 92, 100; Ivan III,
  92-93, *100;* Ivan IV, *93,* 95, 100-101; Lenin,
  role of, 104; Lithuania, 69; 19th Century, *101,*
  103; Peter the Great, 95-98, *96,* 101; Time of
  Troubles, 95, 101; Trotsky and Stalin, 105;
  World War I, 103; World War II, 78, 102, 105
Hitler, Adolf, 105
Horses: gold, Scythian, *100;* Kirgiz, 74
House of the Dead (Dostoyevsky), 120
Housing, 16, *17,* 22, *36-37;* Azerbaijanian, 70;
  childless couple, 23; exchanges, *22,* 23;
  factory-sponsored, *144;* farm workers, 51;
  Irkutsk, 54; middle class, 21-22; in Moscow,
  22-23, *37;* Ukrainian, *52*
Hunters, fur, 54, *55*
Hydroelectric power, 47; Baikal, Lake, 54

I
Icons, *121*
Idiot, The (Dostoyevsky), 122
Income: "long ruble," 57; middle class, 21
Industry, 148-149; Leninsky plant, *143;*
  problems, 150; underground, 152
Infant mortality figures, 20
Inspector General, The (Gogol), 120
Irkutsk, 54; girl guard, *138*
Irrigation, 48, 49-50
Ivan I, Prince of Moscow, 100
Ivan III (the Great), grand duke of Muscovy, 92-
  93, *100*
Ivan IV (the Terrible), Tsar, *93,* 95, 100-101
Ivanov, Dmitri and Sofia, 21-22

J
Jews, 79
Jobs. *See* Work force

K
Kalinin Prospekt, Moscow, *14-15*
Kandinsky, Vasily, 124
Kapitsa, Peter, 22
Kara-Kum desert, *74;* canal through, 73
Kazakhstan, 73
Kerosene-filled piles, building with, 56
KGB (Committee for State Security), 153
Khabarovsk, building construction in, *17*
Khevsur tribesmen, *90-91*
Khrushchev, Nikita, 22, *102,* 140
Kiev, 68-69; family, 21-22; history, 92, 100
Kirgizia and Kirgiz, 74
Kosh-Agach region, *88-89*
Krokodil (humor magazine), 25

L
Labor camps, 153-154
Language, 67-68, 78
Latvians, *61,* 70
Laulupidu (song festival), 70
Lazeishvili, Otari, 71
Leaf, Dr. Alexander, 72

Lenin, Vladimir, 97, *102,* 104-105; quoted, 26,
  45
Lenin Prospekt, maintenance workers on, *8-9*
Leningrad: ballet class, *83;* Summer Palace, *119*
Leninsky Komsomol Automobile Plant, Moscow,
  143-147
Leonov, Leonid, quoted, 54
Lermontov, Mikhail, 119
Life expectancy figures, 20
Link system for school children, 32
Lissitzky, El, poster by, *125*
Literature. *See* Writers
Lithuanians, 69-70
Long-lifers, *72*

M
Magazines, 28; *Krokodil,* 25
Malevich, Kazimir, 124
Mandelstam, Osip, 128, 129
Manufacturing plants, 149; Leninsky plant, *143;*
  problems, 150; underground, 152
Maps: climate, 13; ethnic groups, 70
Marine Resources operation, *151*
Marriages, *31,* 33, *112;* of convenience, 22
Marx, Karl, 139
Matiushin, Mikhail, painting by, *125*
Mental patients, dissidents treated as, *154*
Messerer, Bella and Boris, *130-137*
Middle class, 21-22
Mighty Handful (composers), 126-127
Military expenditures, 149
Military service, 33
Minerals, 46, 47, *chart* 47
Mirkien, Elizabeth, 153
Mislimov, Shirali, 72
Monasteries: Suzdal, 42; Trinity-Saint Sergei,
  Zagorsk, 106; Ukrainian, 108
Monks, *106, 108*
Moscow, 16-17; arts, *127, 128;* baths, 29-30;
  consumer purchasers, 19, *21, 22, 38, 140;*
  fishermen, *41;* in history, 92, 101; housing,
  22-23, *37;* Leninsky plant, *143-147;* Messerer
  family, *130-135;* office buildings, *14-15;*
  parks, *18, 34, 42-43;* residency permits, 22; St.
  Basil's Cathedral, *6-7,* 93; women, *18, 38, 80-*
  81; youth, *25, 127*
Moscow Ice Circus, *23*
Moskva River, *68-69*
Movies, 28-29
Muscovites, 92
Music, composers of, 126-127
Musicians: Latvian, *61;* rock band, *129*
Muslims, *79;* Tartars, 78
Mussorgsky, Modest, 126, 127
"My Country" (Lermontov), quoted, 119

N
Nabokov, Vladimir, quoted, 117
Napoleon Bonaparte, 101, 103
Natural gas, 46; pipeline, *155*
Natural resources, 46-47, *chart* 47
Nenets reindeer herder, *82*
Neryungri, 17
Newspapers, 28

Nicholas I, Tsar, 118
Nicholas II, Tsar, 101, 103, 104
Night on a Bare Mountain (Mussorgsky), 127
Nijinsky, Vaclav, 127
Nixon, Richard, 102
Nomadic reindeer herders, 76, 78
Novelists. *See* Writers
Nuns, *109*
Nutcracker, The (Tchaikovsky), 117, 127

O
October Revolution (1917), 104
Ode to Liberty (Pushkin), 118
Oil reserves, 46
Oleg, Prince, *100*
One Day in the Life of Ivan Denisovich
  (Solzhenitsyn), 120
Oprichnina (secret police), 95, *101*
Orlov, Gregory, 98
Orthodox Church, *106-115;* adoption of, 92

P
Paintings. *See* Art
Palace of Culture, Leninsky plant, 145, *146-*
  147
Palace of Weddings, *31*
Pasternak, Boris, 128-129; grave of, *137*
Peat reserves, 46-47, *48*
Pentecost, observance of, 52
Peredelkino, 131, *136-137*
Permafrost, 55-56; and BAM, *64-65*
Peter of Holstein, 98
Peter the Great, Tsar, 95-98, *96;* ax, *101;*
  Summer Palace, *119*
Petipa, Marius, 127
Pet market, *22*
Petrograd Soviet, 104
Petroleum reserves, 46
Pipeline, natural-gas, *155*
Piukhtitsy, convent at, *109*
Plays: of Chekhov, 126; *The Inspector General,*
  119-120; workers in, *146-147*
Poets and poetry, 128; Akhmadulina, *130-137;*
  Akhmatova, 128; Lermontov, 119;
  Mandelstam, 128, 129; Pushkin, *118*-119;
  Voznesensky, 20; Yevtushenko, 91, 105
Police: KGB, 153; *oprichnina,* 95, *101*
Political organizations, children's, 30
Pollution, water, 48
Possessed, The (Dostoyevsky), 122
Potemkin, Gregory, 99
Prince Igor (opera), 126-127
Private economy, 150; garden plots, 50, 51, *53;*
  underground, 25, 70-71, 152-153
Pugachev (Cossack), 99
Pushkin, Alexander, *118*-119; wife, 118
Pushkin Square, Moscow, *25*

Q
Queues, 20, 26, *38*

R
Railways, 45, 54; Baikal-Amur Mainline, *58-65,*
  149

Rasputin, Gregory, *103*
Recreation, 28-29, *34-35, 40-42;* baths, 29-30; factory workers, 145, *146-147*
Red Army versus White Army, *102,* 104
Reich, Dr. Walter, 154
Reindeer herders, 76, 78, *82*
Religion, *106-115;* ethnic, *79;* history, 92; icons, *121*
Residency permits, 22
Resorts, 29, *40-41*
Rimsky-Korsakov, Nikolai, 126, 127
Rivers, 48; reversal of flow, planned, 49
Rock band, *129*
Romanov, Anastasia, 93, 100-101
Romanov, Tsar Mikhail, 95, 101
Romanov dynasty, 95, 101; Catherine the Great, 98-*99,* 101; culture, attitudes toward, 117, 118; decline and fall, 103-104; Peter the Great, 95-98, *96, 101*
Russians, ethnic, *66,* 67-68; birth rate, 23, 76; history, 91, 92; tensions with non-Russians, 79
Russian Soviet Federated Socialist Republic (R.S.F.S.R.), 67
Russification, 78
Rytkheu, Yuri, 76; quoted, 76, 78

S
Sable hunters, 54, *55*
St. Basil's Cathedral, Moscow, *6-7,* 93
St. Petersburg: building of, 97; Catherine's changes in, 98
Saints Constantine and Helen, Church of, Suzdal, *114-115*
Sakharov, Andrei, 149
Samizdat (self-publishing), 129
Sandunovsky Baths, Moscow, 29-30
Scandinavians in Russian history, 91-92, *100*
Scheherazade (Rimsky-Korsakov), 127
Schools, 32-33
Science, 149; space program, 102, *148*
Scythians, 91; work of, *100*
Security forces: KGB, 153; *oprichnina, 95, 101*
Serfs, 98-99; liberation, *101;* and Turgenev, 124
Ships, factory, for fish processing, *151*
Shopping, *144-145;* department stores, 19; procedure, 26, *38-39*
Shuisky, Andrei, 93
Siberia, 53-54, *55, 56, 88-89;* Akademgorodok, 149; Baikal, Lake, and area, 54-55; building construction, *17,* 56; collective farm, *12-13;* Neryungri, 17; northern frontier, 55-57; pipeline, natural-gas, *155;* railroad construction, *58-65;* windows, *57, 122-123*

Silk Road, Asia, 75
Simis, Konstantin, 152
Slavic peoples. *See* Belorussians; Russians, ethnic; Ukrainians
Sleeping Beauty, The (Tchaikovsky), 127
Slide, wooden, *46*
Socialist Realist painting, *125*
Solzhenitsyn, Alexander, 117, 120, 129; quoted, 153-154
Song festival, Estonian, 70
Soyuz craft, *148*
Space program, *148;* stamp honoring, *102*
Stalin, Josef, *102,* 105, 117, 142; culture, effect on, 127-128; and Khrushchev, 140; labor camps under, 153-154
State farms, *50-51*
Steam baths, 29-30
Stravinsky, Igor, 117, 127
Strugatsky, Boris and Arkady, 129
Sturgeon, 48-49
Summer Palace, Leningrad, *119*
Suzdal: church, *114-115;* monastery, *42*
Swan Lake (Tchaikovsky), 127
Sweden, Russian conflict with, 97

T
Tadzhiks, 73-74
Tamm, Igor, 149
Tartars, 78; in history, 92, 100
Tashkent, 75; street vendor, *88*
Tchaikovsky, Peter Ilyich, 127
Technology, 149
Telephone, *29*
Television, 28; interview for, *133;* news, *26*
Three Sisters, The (Checkhov), 126
Tolstoy, Leo, *116,* 123-124
Topographic features, 45-46
Trans-Siberian Railway, 45, *58-59*
Trinity-Saint Sergei monastery, Zagorsk, *106*
Trotsky, Leon, *102,* 105
Turgenev, Ivan, 124, 126
Turkmenistan and Turkomen, 73, *74*
Tyntareva, Elizabeth, 152

U
Ukraine and Ukrainians, *52,* 68-69, *84-85,* 92; monastery, *108*
Underground operations, 25, 70-71, 152-153
Unions for artists, 127-128
Universities, examinations for, 32-33
Uncle Vanya (Chekhov), 126
Urbanization, 16-17

Uzbekistan and Uzbeks, *67, 73,* 74-75, *79*

V
Vacations, 29, *40-41*
Vegetation zones, 46
Veprintsev, Boris, *32*
Vladimir, Grand Prince of Kiev, 92, *100*
Vodka, use of, *27,* 30
Voinovich, Vladimir, 150
Volga Germans, 78
Volga river, 48
Voznesensky, Andrei, 20

W
Walrus Club members, *69*
War and Peace (Tolstoy), 124
Water power, 47; Baikal, Lake, 54
Water supply, 48; canal, 73; river flow reversal, planned, 49
Weddings, *31,* 33, *112*
White Army versus Red Army, *102,* 104
Windows, Siberian, *57;* frames, *122-123*
Women, role of, *18,* 26-27, *38, 61, 80-81, 83, 86*
Work force, *80-89;* BAM workers, *60-62;* idleness, *142;* Leninsky plant, *143-147;* moonlighting, 25; Siberia, 57, *60-62, 88-89;* women in, 26-27, *61, 80-81, 83, 86, 88*
World War I, 103
World War II, 102, 105; deportations, 78
Writers, 117; Chekhov, 126; Dostoyevsky, 120-122; Gogol, 119-120; Pasternak, 117, 128-129; Solzhenitsyn, 117, 120, 129, 153-154; subterfuge, use of, 129; Tolstoy, *116,* 117, 120, 123-124; Turgenev, 120, 124, 126; union, 128. *See also* Poets and poetry

Y
Yakuts, *60-61*
Yakutsk, 56-57
Yevtushenko, Yevgeni, quoted, 91, 105

Z
Zagorsk religious complex, *106*
Zakharina-Romanov, Anastasia, 93, 100-101

Time-Life Books Inc. offers a wide range of fine recordings, including a *Big Bands* series. For subscription information, call 1-800-621-7026, or write TIME-LIFE MUSIC, Time & Life Building, Chicago, Illinois 60611.